LEGALIZED GAMBLING

A Reference Handbook

LEGALIZED GAMBLING.

A Reference Handbook

William N. Thompson
University of Nevada, Las Vegas

CONTEMPORARY WORLD ISSUES

ABC-CLIO

Santa Barbara, California
Denver, Colorado
Oxford, England

Library of Congress Cataloging-in-Publication Data

Thompson, William Norman.
    Legalized gambling : a reference handbook / William Norman
Thompson.
      p. cm. — (Contemporary world issues)
    Includes bibliographical references and index.
    1. Gambling—Handbooks, manuals, etc. 2. Gambling—United States—
Handbooks, manuals, etc. 3. Gambling—Canada—Handbooks, manuals,
etc.   I. Title. II. Series.
    HV6710.T48   1994   795—dc20   94-21258

ISBN 0-87436-729-8 (alk. paper)

00 99 98 97 96 95   10 9 8 7 6 5 4 3 2

ABC-CLIO, Inc.
130 Cremona Drive, P.O. Box 1911
Santa Barbara, California 93116-1911

This book is printed on acid-free paper ∞ .
Manufactured in the United States of America

This book is dedicated to John, I. Nelson, Bill, Judy, Henry, Tony, Andrew, Michele, Arnie, Keith, Ricardo, and Susan—pioneers, colleagues, and friends in gaming research.

Contents

List of Figures and Tables

Preface

ACCORDING TO CHARLES T. CLOTFELTER and Philip J. Cook in their book *Selling Hope: State Lotteries in America,* Thomas Jefferson once called gambling "a wonderful thing"—a tax that is assessed "only on the willing." Jefferson suggested that gambling activities might have positive results for governments that could not levy direct taxes for certain purposes. Moreover, the purchase of a lottery ticket, according to Jefferson, need not be painful as the price does not result in any "sensible injury."

Jefferson's words were certainly subject to debate in 1826 when they were written, and they are debatable now; but the words of the author of the Declaration of Independence were used at the time to persuade a single legislative body to approve a single drawing. Jefferson's wisdom in advocating these so-called painless taxes has now become almost doctrine for many politicians and voters across Canada and the United States—in state after state and province after province the North American continent is eagerly attempting to legalize all forms of gambling—lotteries, casinos, bingo games, and wagering on races and sports events. A gaming industry that has met with approval from Wall Street investment firms only in recent years is now actively seeking alliances with political leaders who face budget deficits and fear the consequences they will face if they have to increase taxes.

All 10 Canadian provinces and 48 of the states now permit some form of legalized gambling—and all are entertaining proposals for more gambling. The rush to legalize gambling in North America is gaining momentum; some people compare it to that of a powerful freight train heading down the railroad tracks, promising solutions to public fiscal problems. The solutions are only a ride away, they say, but the solutions will not be found unless we jump on the train and jump on it quickly, because soon the train will be gone. Along with the notion that governments can solve their financial problems "painlessly" with gambling is the promise that this kind of commercial enterprise will bring jobs to communities where unemployment lines are growing.

As good as it all may seem, other voices suggest that the promises of gambling are false promises, and they warn governments not to become hooked on the narcotic-like force of sanctioned gaming—the tax revenues promised by gambling might not be there and the bite of the taxes that do come from voluntary gambling may not be without consequence. Many citizens feel the pain of legalized gambling—poor people drawn into a quest for a ticket out of an impoverished existence, or weak personalities who can not let go of the notion that there is "something for nothing" and who let gambling become their compulsion. Opponents of legalized gambling point out that job creation and economic development may be as elusive as the idea that gambling brings free money to government coffers. These voices are also eager to suggest that a myriad of criminal activity accompanies the legalization of gambling—and that some of the activity is conducted by organized criminals.

Proponents of legalized gambling see many winners in the activity, while opponents see losers and victims. Actually, Thomas Jefferson was not an unabashed advocate of lotteries. In an earlier statement than that referred to above, he suggested that he never bought tickets, and could therefore never ask others to buy tickets. So, perhaps, Jefferson started the debate over legalized gambling in the United States by representing both sides of the argument— but his debates with himself were probably cool and wise. The current debates over the legalization of gambling are heating up, and today there may be more smoke and heat than there is light. Legalized gambling is emerging as one of the leading issues of the 1990s. This handbook attempts to take a close look at the many arguments for and against the legalization of gambling. It also presents a comprehensive historical background to the issues, along with many resource materials that will be useful to both the citizen wishing to become more familiar with the subject and to students seeking to develop in-depth research projects on the issue.

This book is organized to provide ready access to a broad range of information about legalized gambling. Chapter 1 gives a historical overview of gambling in North America, describes the roles of government in gambling and the various perceptions of gambling in society, and identifies the current issues and debates surrounding legalized gambling. Chapter 2 provides a chronology of significant events pertaining to gambling from the arrival of the first colonists in North America to the present. Chapter 3 provides brief biographies of famous individuals from the rich history of legalized gambling. Chapter 4 provides a legal framework on legalized gambling in North America as well as specific points of view and statistics. Chapter 5 is a directory of organizations, both private and government operated, in North America. Chapter 6 lists print resources for further study of gaming, and chapter 7 lists nonprint resources and contains both feature films and documentaries. Finally, a glossary details relevant terms from gambling.

A powerful train is loose. It may or may not be on firm tracks, and we cannot be sure of the direction in which it is headed. But the train is moving, and we cannot hope to control it unless we understand those sitting in the cab and unless we understand the fuels propelling it and the physics of its engine. The gambling train must be controlled. Control will come only if we approach the train with knowledge. It is the author's desire that this handbook may encourage the quest for that knowledge.

Acknowledgments

ALL PROJECTS THAT INVOLVE gathering, synthesizing, and presenting research materials must necessarily be collective efforts. While this reference handbook lists only one author, I am very mindful of the influence of others and the work they put into gaming research—work that truly has been the *sine qua non* of this project. Without the help of others, this project could not have reached fruition.

At the outset I wish to dedicate my efforts, which culminated in the following pages, to a core group of individuals who have inspired my recent academic career—a career that has been focused upon investigations of various aspects of the gambling phenomenon. I met John Dombrink while we were both working in a political campaign in Nevada in 1982. Soon I learned of his doctoral study on the efforts to legalize casinos in New Jersey and Florida. That study was truly a launching pad for my first research paper in gaming—a study of efforts to get casinos into new jurisdictions across the United States. Soon John and I were working together on a book manuscript, which we called *The Last Resort: Success and Failure in Campaigns for Casinos*. John also helped guide my career as we collaborated on writing the *Gambling Report* for the President's Commission on Organized Crime. Always in our studies—and all my later studies as well—I could turn for advice to I. Nelson Rose, author of *Gambling and the Law*, and truly a pioneer in scholarly work on the subject of gaming.

My research, as well as that of all others in the gaming field, has received inspirational as well as solid academic support from Bill Eadington, who very accurately would be described as the founder of a discipline of gambling studies in the world. Beginning in the 1970s, Bill organized international conferences on gambling research, and he has been a catalyst, bringing together former strangers who share a fascination for this topic of inquiry. Bill also publishes papers from his conferences, and he now serves with Editor Henry Lesieur on the editorial staff of the academic journal of our discipline, formerly *Journal of Gaming Behavior,* now the *Journal of Gaming Research.* Editor Lesieur's encouragement in my work has been immeasurable. The bottom line is that Henry allowed me to publish so that my efforts in this field would not perish. Bill Eadington also created the Institute for the Study of Gambling and Commercial Gaming at the University of Nevada, Reno. At the institute, he is ably assisted by Judy Cornelius, who has helped propel all of our fraternity of gaming professor-types onward with her encouragement and her organizational and editorial talents.

Tony Cabot of the Lionel, Collins, and Sawyer Law Firm in Las Vegas presented me with a tremendous opportunity to blend research materials gathered in my travels to casinos in Europe, Central America, and South America, along with his knowledge about gaming laws in North America. Together we joined with colleague Andrew Tottenham, a London gaming consultant, as editors of a collection of essays on casino gaming laws in each of 80 jurisdictions around the world. Our book is entitled *International Casino Law.* It is published by Bill Eadington's Institute for the Study of Gambling and Commercial Gaming.

My dedication to Michele Comeau is in thanks for working with me in developing customer service training programs for the gaming industry. Our book, *Casino Customer Service—The WIN WIN Game,* has enabled me to add a critical dimension to my interaction with executives and employees in the gaming industry. Arnie Wexler has been a pioneer in sounding the clarion call for awareness and understanding about social problems that surround gambling activity. He eagerly gives his energies to scholars examining problem gambling. I appreciate Arnie taking his time to talk with me and my classes when he comes to Las Vegas.

Keith Schwer is the director of the Center for Business and Economic Research at the University of Nevada, Las Vegas, and he serves as the chair of the First Interstate Bank (FIB) research committee for the College of Business and Economics. The bank has been generous with grant money that has supported my research efforts in the gaming field. I am indebted to FIB, and to the University of Nevada Sabbatical Research Fund for important encouragement in my gaming research career. Keith Schwer has also facilitated my career by allowing me to have released time from class duties so that I can work on center projects that analyze facets of the gaming industry. I am also indebted to Ricardo Gazel, professor of economics and associate director of the center, for providing me with enlightenment and insights into the economic aspects of the dynamic growing gaming industry. As all of my colleagues know, along with the growing members of the gaming research fraternity, none of us could do our tasks adequately without the assistance of Susan Jarvis, who manages the Special Collections Gaming Library on our Las Vegas campus and always eagerly responds to letters and phone calls besieging her daily from all points on the globe.

To these pioneers in gaming research, these colleagues in my research projects, and these friends—John, I. Nelson, Bill, Judy, Henry, Tony, Andrew, Michele, Arnie, Keith, Ricardo, and Susan—I dedicate this book.

To others I also extend my warmest thanks for assistance and encouragement. I owe no small measure of gratitude to Graduate Assistant Grace Chen Skelly of our College of Business and Economics for countless hours of running back and forth to our very special gaming library. I must also thank college staff members for manuscript and copying assistance—to Sharon Green, Donna Evans, Patricia Ray Roach, Diana Sjoberg—thank you.

Projects never seem to progress in the logical planned way they were intended. This project was to be a quick overview assessment of my favorite topic. I assured the editors of ABC-CLIO that indeed I could have a document finished in a year's time. I am only thankful that they encouraged me and stuck with me, allowing new deadlines as unrealistic old deadlines passed me by. I hung in there (and really took only an extra year) not on my own, but as a result of the steady but always positive prodding of Henry Rasof and Todd Hallman. They made it happen, and I am so happy that they stuck with me. Henry and Todd—my deepest thanks.

As I have learned with my other gaming research projects, I am addressing a fast-changing industry in this book. Events are changing the gaming landscape in North America almost daily. Accordingly, when the words of this book are set into their final printed copy, many of the words will be outdated. We have to expect this. The gaming field is also a very complex field replete with many controversies. More research can always lead to better insights. However, my efforts have been bounded by both time and my own energy levels. Inevitably, the reader will discover areas where I wrote too quickly, or I wrote without proper reflection. Regrettably, I accept that this will be the case. I cannot apologize for the rapid changes occurring in the industry, but I must apologize for factual inaccuracies that may be discovered. While I could never have written the book without the help of many others—those named above and others unnamed—I must give credit to these others for all good scholarship found in these pages—it is I alone who must shoulder blame for any and all errors.

Not to end this section negatively—I hope the reader can discover some of the fun I had in bringing together ideas and information on my favorite research topic—legalized gambling.

1

Introduction

THE EDITORS OF *ESQUIRE* MAGAZINE have called it "the world's second oldest diversion." (Newman 1962) *Business Week* said it was America's "newest growth industry" (26 June 1978) and pronounced in a cover story that a fever for it was sweeping the nation. (Welles 24 April 1989) Indeed, the figures bear this out. Voters and politicians endorse it more and more. It is gambling, an industry which today is embroiled in governmental issues across the North American continent.

Gambling has become a "front burner" political issue for many reasons. State, local, and provincial governments face serious budget shortfalls, the kind of which have not been witnessed since the Great Depression of the 1930s, and the public has been engulfed in a general antitaxation movement that has blocked political approval of traditional sources for new revenues. The public also appears to be softening its objections to a variety of "sins," such as gambling and adult consensual nonmarital sexual activities formerly termed as "victimless crimes." Moreover, the gaming industry has attracted entrepreneurs eager for new markets and high yields on their investments. The gaming industry willingly sponsors political campaigns for gambling legalization.

Just a few decades ago, legalized gambling was confined to the casinos found in one isolated state, plus a few other places that allowed wagers on horse races or charity bingo games. Then came the 1960s, and, starting with New Hampshire, state after state turned to public lotteries as a way of generating tax revenue. Canadian provinces followed suit. In addition, many jurisdictions began to open doors wider for charity gambling, and horse tracks began to penetrate all parts of the continent. When voters in New Jersey authorized casinos for Atlantic City in 1976, many felt the lid of restriction had come off.

Casino gaming was not accepted like other forms of gambling were until the late 1980s. (Dombrink and Thompson 1990) During this period South Dakota and Colorado opened certain historical locations to casino activity with limited betting, and Iowa and Illinois approved casino games on riverboats. These examples became models for duplication elsewhere. Indian reservations entered the gambling picture when they began to recognize unique legal status that exempted them from many state restrictions. Reservation leaders discovered that bingo and even casino-type games could generate large sums of moneys for tribal programs.

Gambling may be defined as an activity in which a person subjects something of value—usually money—to a risk involving a large element of chance in the hopes of winning something of greater value, which is usually more money. The types of gambling addressed in this handbook have all been addressed by policy makers: bingo, lotteries, raffles, dice, card games, slot machines, and sporting events, including team games, individual contests, and horse or dog races. While gambling encompasses all these activities, the term "gaming" is usually associated with the activities found in casinos. Sports and race betting, on the other hand, are commonly referred to as "wagering." Herein, the terms "gambling," "gaming," and "wagering" will be used somewhat interchangeably.

Throughout our lives we take chances in the hopes of obtaining certain rewards. We do this when we select our study areas in college, when we accept jobs, and when we go into business. Certainly we are taking chances when we invest in the stock markets, or even when we deposit money into savings accounts. All these enterprises involve the risk of valuable time, money, and opportunity in exchange for the chance to reap a reward. On the nonfinancial front, we may risk our health—even our lives—in the pursuit of recreation. These risks include activities like skiing, contact sports, scuba diving, bungy jumping, or car racing. We also assume risks seeking the pleasures of food, or seeking to fulfill other appetites. This handbook does not concern itself with these types of gambles, although the information presented may contribute to the understanding of such activity. Our attention, rather, will be focused on commercial (including charitable and government-sponsored) games involving a considerable element of chance.

Some form of legalized gambling exists now in 48 states in the United States and in each of the Canadian provinces. Bingo games are legal in 47 states, the District of Columbia, and all Canadian provinces. (*Gaming and Wagering Business* September–October 1993; Thompson 1994) Lotteries are conducted by 37 state governments, the District of Columbia, and all the provinces. Horse race betting is permitted in 42 states; 19 states allow dog race wagering, and 4 states permit betting on jai alai games. All the Canadian provinces have some form of horse race betting. Nevada, New Jersey, and more than a dozen other states and eight of the ten provinces offer some form of slot machine, card room, or casino-type games. Major land-based casinos are in place in Nevada, Atlantic City, New Jersey, and Winnipeg, Manitoba.

If all the gaming activities permitted in United States jurisdictions were brought together under a single holding company, that company would collect revenues making it the nation's nineteenth largest corporation. More than $329 billion is gambled each year in the United States (Canadians wager an additional $6 billion), and legal gaming organizations—lotteries, tracks, casinos, and bingo halls—retain almost $30 billion gross in gaming wins. (Christiansen 1993) Considering that the win figure represents gross sales, our holding company would lag behind the three biggest automakers, IBM, and AT&T, but surge ahead of corporate giants like K-Mart and American Express.

Although gambling has always existed, public involvement in the activity has not occurred evenly throughout history. There have been eras of gambling suppression and prohibition and eras of permissiveness. Today we are most certainly experiencing a movement away from suppression and toward greater leniency. How did we arrive at this condition, and why is legalized gambling expanding and receiving more and more political attention?

Gambling throughout History

The editors of *Esquire* wrote that the "oldest diversion . . . is the same as the oldest profession, but it's odds-on that gambling came next, perhaps even immediately afterwards." (Newman 1962)

Others, however, may disagree with this placement of gambling on the timeline of mankind. The authors of *The Business of Risk: Commercial Gambling in Mainstream America* suggest that gambling should be listed as the starting point of "sinful" activity. Abt, Smith, and Christiansen portray Adam and Eve's choice to eat forbidden fruit in the Garden of Eden as humankind's first real gamble. The price of this failed wager, they say, was a loss of innocence: "To many, man's fall from grace and subsequent history are proof [that] it [eating fruit] was immoral, or a sucker bet, the first step down the road to ruin. . . . To others, the wager was an act of self-actualization." Through the Garden of Eden gamble, they assert, "Adam and Eve acquired humanity," and society began. (Abt, Smith, and Christiansen 1985)

The mortal souls of all societies throughout history have known gambling. Compulsive gamblers in biblical Egypt were sent to quarries to work off their debts. When archaeologists excavated the pyramids, they found dice beside the mummified bodies of pharaohs—dice that were shaved, or "crooked." Greek history contains stories of soldiers who shot craps to while away the monotonous hours during the siege of Troy, and the Bible documents the story of Roman centurions gambling for the robes of Christ following the crucifixion. The Old and New Testaments, indeed, contain many references to gambling.

Roman society generally precluded the masses from gaming, except during festivals. However, gambling was a regular part of life in retirement communities established near hot springs and natural bath waters for career military personnel in the far reaches of Europe. Long before the Renaissance period, Germans and Englishmen wagered at Spa, Baden, and Bath. The privileged classes in Rome also gambled away their considerable leisure time. It is just as likely that Nero was raffling off slaves or villas to his palace guests as it is that he was playing a fiddle when Rome burned in A.D. 64. (Scarne 1961)

During the Middle Ages, pilgrims traveling to Canterbury, traders, and soldiers moving east to the Crusades utilized old Roman roads. Inns along the way provided for their comfort, food, lodging, and entertainment. These inns also became the centers for gambling in communities on these routes. Monarchs during the Middle Ages wagered on the speed of their horses. It is known that the England's infamous King John (1199–1216) kept special racing horses in his Royal stables. (Scarne 1961)

Various kinds of gambling implements, such as sticks and dice, existed in the earliest societies, but playing cards can be traced to more recent origins. Cards probably appeared in Asia shortly after the Chinese invented paper in the first or second century A.D. The first European card decks date to fourteenth-century Italy and France. The popularity of card games spread rapidly throughout Europe after this time, and there is no doubt but that Columbus brought cards to the Western Hemisphere on his first voyage in 1492.

Continental lotteries financed public improvements prior to European migrations to North America. The first lotteries probably were held during the Roman Empire, while the first government-organized lottery took place in Florence in 1530. Soon afterwards, lottery drawings occurred in Venice and Genoa. The Italians introduced lotteries to the French in 1533 when Catherine de Medici travelled to Versailles to marry King Henry II. Queen Elizabeth authorized England's first lottery in 1566 (although the drawing was not held until 1569). (Blanche 1950) The money secured by the Queen was dedicated "towardes the reparation of the havens [harbors for ships] and strength of the Realme and towardes such other publique good works." (Scarne 1961)

When European settlers came to the New World they brought gambling paraphernalia and a gambling tradition. They quickly discovered that the indigenous people of the continent participated in a variety of gaming activities as well. Native Americans wagered heavily on sporting events. Favorite team games included lacrosse and a precursor of modern-day football. The teams were comprised of young males from neighboring villages or tribes. Supporters of each team wagered their possessions by placing blankets, clothing, jewelry, pottery, weapons, and livestock on a line near the middle of a playing field. Native Americans also bet on foot races, horse races, and athletic contests involving various hunting and warring skills. A popular contest involved shooting arrows into a rolling hoop.

Dice games were also popular. Early American dice typically was played with flat stones or bones painted with different colors on each side. Players would choose colors as the dice were thrown in the air. Also prevalent were guessing games involving deception. In one, a team would conceal a small object behind its collective back and pass it from member to member. The opposite team would then try to guess which member possessed the object.

These games and contests could last for days, with players and bettors engaged until they fell over from exhaustion. While no "credit" gambling was allowed, a player's total possessions could be put at risk in the betting. Often, a series of double-or-nothing wagers would "wipe out" a participant. However, winners normally returned sufficient possessions so that losers would not face destitution or injury from exposure to the elements.

Gambling activity has ebbed and flowed with varying intensities throughout history. In what has appeared to be a love-hate relationship between the public and gambling promoters, several "waves" of permissiveness have rippled through North America, only to subside with prohibitionary regulation.

Gaming authority I. Nelson Rose suggests that we are now in the "third wave" of gaming in European-American history. The first occurred during the colonial era and early years of nationhood. Lotteries, horse racing, and gentlemanly card games punctuated this phase. Captain John Smith's Virginia encountered financial problems almost immediately after European settlers arrived at Jamestown Colony, and in his desperation for funding, Smith obtained a charter from King James in 1612 to conduct a lottery in London. (Chafetz 1960) Soon, lotteries were being played in America as well, and becoming an integral element in colonial development. Lotteries were used to supplement government treasuries and were engaged by private organizations. Churches, and colleges such as Harvard, Princeton, Columbia, and Rutgers, used lotteries to finance construction projects. In fact, the Revolutionary War itself was financed in part by a lottery established by the Continental Congress.

Newly formed state governments used lotteries to fund military activity, and later turned to this funding mechanism for internal improvements after winning independence from the Crown. One report estimates that, between 1790 and 1860, 24 of 33 states financed buildings, roads, and bridges from lottery revenues. This era peaked in 1831, when eight states ran 420 lottery games that sold more than $66 million in tickets. This sum was five times that of the federal budget that year. However, lotteries were soon afflicted with scandals and swindles and lost public support. The emergence of Andrew Jackson as the dominant national leader and promoter of governmental reform also energized the detractors of government-operated gambling operations. State after state abolished lotteries and prohibited private parties from selling tickets. By the time of the Civil War, which effectively marked the end of the first gambling wave, only three states permitted lotteries.

Riverboat gaming began in the early 1800s as commerce moved into the Mississippi Valley. Robert Fulton placed a steamboat on the river in 1812. Soon, cardsharps were in business, fleecing unsuspecting farmers and merchants who had to use the boats to get their products to market. In the 1830s and 1840s, reformers effectuated the closing of many gambling operations on boats and in river towns from St. Louis to New Orleans.

The first wave also carried horse racing to the eastern half of the continent, although greater gambling activity was found in the South. Race horses had arrived in Virginia by 1620. Circular courses were laid out in New York as early as 1665 and were quickly imitated elsewhere. Wagering on horse races was, at first, an activity that took place among gentlemen, and was considered more of a sporting matter than true gambling. Similarly, the "landed gentry" engaged in poker games, while general gambling among the working classes was prohibited.

Restrictions were imposed on gambling almost from the beginning of the Colonial period. Plymouth Colony, for example, banned card playing as early as 1621—only a year after the arrival of the Pilgrims. Similar bans were applied to other popular games and to gaming at popular locations, such as taverns. Such gaming was seen as destructive to the Protestant work ethic, and a contributor to idleness and debauchery. Nonetheless, simultaneous to such bans, society endorsed lotteries, horse racing, and games among the rich throughout this period. America's initial flirtations with gambling ended with the Civil War. Horses were needed for wartime activities, and racing had come to be viewed as wasteful. During these years, southern gentry faced the loss of not only its social position, but also its land. There was no time for poker, and the scandals of earlier lottery years had destroyed public appetites for that pastime.

Following the Civil War, a second wave of gambling began as devastated state and local governments searched for funding. Again, they turned to the lottery. Horse racing also regained popularity, as did card games on the western frontier. A number of southern states turned to the lottery in the Reconstruction Era, but only one survived after 1878—the notorious Louisiana Lottery. Ticket sales were authorized by the Louisiana Legislature, promoted by bribery, and run by a New York syndicate. The lottery thrived because it was the only one in the country and it merchandised tickets through the mail. The Louisiana Lottery became the target of a national reform movement, and Congress subsequently passed a law in 1890 prohibiting the sale of lottery tickets through the mail. The state legislature shut down the lottery games two years later.

The Gold Rush and silver strikes in the West drew fortune seekers by the tens of thousands. Gamblers who had been stifled by eastern reformers now had an alternative location to ply their trade. Gambling in gold and silver camps became a major entertainment activity for prospectors, miners, and cowboys, with opulent gaming houses springing up in San Francisco, Denver, and Colorado Springs. As gambling dives permeated the mining boom towns and camps of the West, laws were enacted to stop the activity. A lack of law enforcement personnel, however, ensured that most of the regulations would remain unenforced. Simply maintaining civil order was a major task for the police. At this time, gaming houses also emerged in the East as the first vestiges of organized crime began to recognize the possibilities of offering games of chance to the upper classes.

Many such houses were tolerated until another series of reforms smashed the nation's second major era of legalized gambling. The first decade of the twentieth century witnessed Arizona and New Mexico Territories banning gambling in the hopes of winning support for statehood. As mining activity subsided, so did the demand for gambling. This trend bolstered the ability of lawmen to enforce gambling regulations. Nevada finally closed its casinos in 1910, and all but a very few of the states banned wagers on horse races. For the most part, legal gambling lay dormant after this period for several years. In the 1930s, legal casinos returned to Nevada and horse racing returned to 21 states. These states, facing major budget problems related to their Depression economies, charted a trend of expanding track wagering which continued through the 1940s. Other states began permitting charity bingo games in the 1950s, and Florida began to allow bets on jai alai games. Lotteries, however, were not poised to enjoy rehabilitated legal status until the New Hampshire legislature passed a sweepstakes law in 1963.

With the initiation of the New Hampshire Lottery in 1964, a third wave of legalized gambling swept the nation. New York soon approved a lottery; New Jersey followed suit. In 1969 Canada amended its criminal code to allow lotteries in provinces and to authorize charitable gaming. Every province moved to establish lotteries in the 1970s, and a variety of charitable and governmental gaming schemes led Manitoba, Ontario, and Quebec to open full-fledged casinos. Eventually in the United States, 37 states and the District of Columbia authorized lotteries, and even more states authorized bets on horse or dog races. In 1976 New Jersey voters approved casinos for Atlantic City. While casino gaming failed to spread at first, the issue of legalizing casinos in the 1990s is very much at the top of the political agendas in a dozen or more states. Limited casino gaming and riverboat gaming has been approved for eight additional states, with operations already underway. Gambling has taken on a new dimension as Native American reservations in the United States and Canada have opened bingo halls and casinos in 9 provinces and 30 states. Of all the Canadian and United States jurisdictions, only Hawaii and Utah authorize no legal gambling.

Riding the Crest of the Third Wave

Why does legalized gambling continue to spread? The most salient answer can be expressed in a single phrase: *the economic imperative.* There is a lot of money to be made in gambling. Operators of gaming establishments can be especially well positioned if they can maneuver themselves into a monopoly position for even a brief period of time. Governments perceive that they can reap financial benefits from gaming as direct operators or as tax collectors. Other entrepreneurs benefit from just being near gambling establishments. These business people can sell goods to establishments or gaming customers.

While there is evidence to suggest that people are more willing to support legalization efforts than they were in the past, overwhelming public demand for legalization does not exist. In marketing terms, it might be appropriate to conclude that legalization is not being "pulled" by public demand. Rather, it appears that entrepreneurs are "pushing" the spread of gaming.

Game operators, whether legal or illegal, salivate when they recall the opening of the Resorts International Casino in Atlantic City on Memorial Day weekend in 1978. This was the only casino in Atlantic City then, and indeed the only casino in America east of Nevada. Resorts International maintained a monopoly status for more than a year. People waited hours at the casino door while the fire marshall tried to monitor the surging crowds. But they were hardly successful. Gaming writer Ovid Demaris describes the action:

> Customers were jammed twenty deep at the tables, aisles and slot machines were jammed, the casino was blue with smoke. The noise level of the 900 slot machines, of gamblers exhorting their dice, and of music blaring from the cocktail lounge had reached a numbing crescendo, but no one wanted to leave. . . . People with money clutched in their fists pushed and shoved and fought for a chance to get at a table. (Demaris 1986)

Before the first day of action ended the casino had won over a million dollars from these "lucky" players. Within nine months, Resorts International paid for its entire $77 million capital investment. (Smith 1986)

Such stories help foment entrepreneurial dreams in this industry. A common wishful thought is: "Oh, to just have a monopoly operation." Similar successes on Indian reservations encourage investors to enter contracts wherein they pay for all capital and operating expenses and allow the tribes to reap 60 percent of net profits for seven years. After that time the entire investment is transferred to the tribes. Hopes for extraordinary windfall profits cause operators who complain about $6^{1}/_{4}$ percent gross win taxes in Nevada to eagerly apply for monopoly licenses in New Orleans that carry $18^{1}/_{2}$ percent tax levies.

The experience of many companies with gambling products over the past two decades has convinced the sectors of the economy with capital control that gambling represents a good investment. As banks, stock equity markets, and bond markets open to gambling investors, more entrepreneurs see the industry as a viable option. On Wall Street, gambling has became legitimate.

It has not been only the casino and games operators who have garnered major profits from gambling. Several companies have become very successful by supplying needed products to the industry. For instance, International Gaming Technology pioneered the development of the video poker machine. With the spread of gaming in the 1980s and 1990s, this company has realized soaring profits. Its investors have seen stock prices double, split, and double again.

Similarly, Scientific Games has profited handsomely from the spread of lottery games into new jurisdictions. The company prints instant lottery tickets and manufactures other lottery supplies. The biggest company in its market, Scientific Games is well positioned to win contracts for its products when a new lottery is created. In 1984 the firm invested $2 million in a lottery campaign for California, but the company's efforts to win votes went beyond the mere investment of money. Scientific Games actually wrote the ballot proposition!

After the campaign was over, it was clear that only one company could meet the specifications set forth for suppliers in the ballot proposal: Scientific Games. In an effort to find rival companies, state officials extended the bidding period, but to no avail. Scientific Games won an initial contract worth $40 million to supply tickets during the first year of lottery operation.

In their effort to unilaterally "drive" the legalized gambling market, entrepreneurs have wielded a major force in their strategic equation. Just as manufacturers of other products push their merchandise by activating wholesalers and retailers, gambling interests mobilize politicians to obtain the legal support necessary. Political players may see legalization as beneficial to their personal careers, especially during times of economic stress. The 1980s and 1990s witnessed an array of economic crises in state and local governments. Jobs were lost to international competition and to falling prices in certain sectors of the economy, such as the oil industry. State tax bases were eroded. At the same time, a federal budget crisis led Washington officials to cut aid to state and local governments while demanding that states assume operational and financial control of both old and new programs. All this has occurred in tandem with general anti-tax sentiments on the part of the public. Voters are crying out, "Read our lips! We will pay no new taxes!"

A Painless Tax

Stated simply, states need new revenues at a time when the public is unwilling to accept new tax measures. The federal option of permitting deficits to grow is not available to most states, which have constitutional provisions that demand balanced budgets. The option of drastically cutting state services is not politically feasible. Politicians turn either to taxes or to major budget cuts and find themselves without defenses at election time. It is a dilemma with few appealing solutions, save for one: legalized gambling. With this alternative, government revenues can be enhanced and public service programs can be maintained. Moreover, taxes do not have to be hiked—at least those levied directly upon voters. Governor Ann Richards of Texas put it succinctly: "It's a question of money. Either we get it from a lottery or we'll get it from a huge tax bill." (*Gaming and Wagering Business* September–October 1991)

We will discuss the viability of raising revenue through gambling below. It may be suggested that this is not an ideal solution to state and local fiscal crises, and it is understood that most politicians realize the limitations of relying too much on this revenue source; but it is a revenue source that has political acceptability. After all, a politician's major need is to buy time, and gambling helps by providing immediate help in resolving many of today's fiscal crises.

The appeals of gambling companies are made to politicians in many ways. Each month Scientific Games purchases a full page slick color advertisement on the back cover of *Gaming and Wagering Business,* the leading trade publication for the gaming industry. Throughout most of 1985, the advertisement featured a large map of the United States and a headline which read: WHAT IT COSTS YOUR STATE BY NOT JOINING THE LOTTERY MAJORITY. In the advertisement, each state without a lottery has a figure above it representing the amount of money lost by not instituting a lottery. The numbers used in this advertisement, recorded in Figure 1.1, range from $14 million dollars for Alaska to $480 million for Texas.

The advertisement apparently appealed to state officials. In truth, the numbers represented were quite conservative, as many states came to realize. But the ad was successful. Fifteen of the 28 states included have since established lotteries. (*Gaming and Wagering Business* June 1985)

The Spread of Gambling

For many legalization efforts, the combination of entrepreneurial drive and sympathetic public officials is all that is needed for success. However, even where legislators and governors are free to make gaming decisions without voter endorsement, they appear reluctant to do so without some consideration of public attitude. As leaders have tested the waters of public opinion a growing acceptance of gambling has been detected, specifically the notion that states should permit residents to freely participate in gambling activities.

FIGURE 1.1
Potential Revenues for Non-Lottery States (1985)

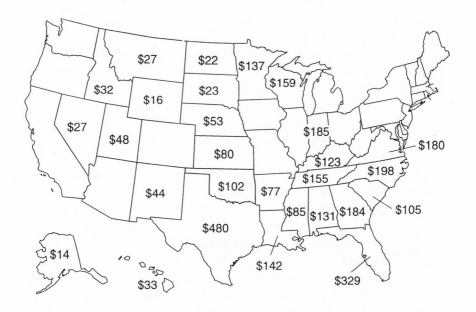

Figures in millions

Source: "What it Cost Your State by Not Joining the Lottery Majority," Advertising. Backcover, *Gaming and Wagering Business*, June 1985.

The era of expanded legalized gambling has coincided with a trend toward increased permissiveness in society. There certainly is a connection between attitudes about lifestyle, sex, pornography—even abortion and occasional drug use—and attitudes toward gambling. The notion that government has no business in our bedrooms relates to the notion that government has no business telling us how to spend our leisure time and our own money as long as we are doing so without coercion or harm to others.

A snowballing effect occurs when numbers of jurisdictions endorse the legalization of particular forms of gambling. A map (see chapter 4) showing the dates when states and provinces established lotteries illustrates this. Similarly, the order in which midwestern states bordering the Mississippi River and its tributaries endorsed riverboat gaming provides a good example of the phenomenon. Jurisdictions imitate one another in hopes of preventing their neighbors from taking business away from them. Imitation also occurs when jurisdictional neighbors can observe gaming operations in a way that they lose moral inhibitions regarding gambling. Such observance enables them to become familiar with regulatory frameworks and consequences.

The one time when a snowball did not get rolling was immediately after the Atlantic City casino legalization. Following that episode, neighboring jurisdictions were presented with a very negative picture of wide-open casino activity. Inability of the Atlantic City casinos to effectuate community renewal in terms of housing, jobs, and quality of life—accompanied by suggestions of organized crime involvement with political decision-making regarding casinos and evidence of increased street crime—led neighboring officials to reject the promised benefits of casino gaming. (Dombrink and Thompson 1990)

Throughout the 1980s a number of jurisdictions rejected casinos, while other locales succeeded in establishing lotteries. The negative consequences of lotteries apparently have not been as easy to observe, nor have the negative aspects of limited casino gaming in mountain towns or on riverboats. The same public which appears to harbor apprehension about Las Vegas-style gaming seems to accept casinos if they are floated from local river docks or tucked unobtrusively away in mountain towns.

In sum, the times have ripened for the spread of gaming, and entrepreneurs appear to be at the ready to meet market demand with plenty of commercial ventures.

Government in the Gaming Enterprise

Governments play a variety of roles that pertain to gambling. Five basic roles—from prohibition and toleration, to regulation and actual management of gaming—are presented in the discussion below.

Government Prohibition

Almost all governments at some time play the role of gambling prohibitor. Indeed, we can even find the following passage in the constitution of the state of Nevada, the sole jurisdiction in America that has established gaming as its primary industry: "No lottery shall be authorized by this State, nor shall the sale of lottery tickets be allowed" (Article IV, Section 24). Methods of enforcing gambling prohibition range from vigorous policing with special vice units to minimal concern—even de facto law enforcement toleration of illegal activity.

Legal prohibitions of gambling activity probably predate biblical times. In our own legal tradition they can be traced to the Middle Ages. Richard I of England prohibited gambling—except for royalty—in the twelfth century. Parliament passed the first law on gambling in 1388. (Rose 1986) The first English settlers in America confronted a need to control gambling. In 1624 the Virginia House of Burgesses commanded that ministers should not spend their "tyme idelie by day or by night, playing dice, cards, or any unlawful game." In 1630 the Puritan Colony of Massachusetts Bay recognized that gambling was a problem for its population and ordered that "all persons whatsoever that have cards, dice, or tables in their houses shall make away with them before the next court under punishment of pain." (Berger and Bruning 1979)

While gambling is a serious policy issue, prohibition efforts have at times entered the realm of the ridiculous. For instance, the Key West, Florida, City Council passed a resolution making it illegal to bet on a turtle race, while Mirror Lake, New Hampshire, banned wagers on rat or mice fights. A North Dakota law once banned gambling while consuming pretzels and beer, and Corvallis, Oregon, determined that women could not gamble while having coffee. The town of Callicon, New York, stipulated that no gambling should take place in a barber's chair, and Lemon Springs, North Carolina, ruled that it was illegal to make wagers within four hours after eating onions or garlic. (Pelton 1980)

Like the frivolous stipulations above, most jurisdictions have restricted only selected gaming activities. Only Utah and Hawaii have total bans on all gambling, and gambling referendums are appearing on election ballots across North America.

Government Toleration

Governments often play a second role—that of passive observer. In these cases, government sits on the sidelines and allows private social gambling without regulation or oversight. Under the common law of England—a body of court decisions that were often observed in America—gambling was permissible unless a legislative body had declared otherwise. (Rose 1986)

Nonetheless, British authorities stopped the games when they became disorderly and courts intervened if disputes arose between betting parties. In fact, considerable legal attention was devoted during the colonial period to lawsuits involving horse race gamblers. Early courts were also asked to assist gamblers in collection of money owed them by other gamblers; but in 1710 the English Parliament passed the Statute of Anne, which declared that gambling debts could not be collected through the courts. Since then, the issue of suing to recover winnings has been debated in many American jurisdictions, but it was not until 1983 that Nevada elected to allow gambling debt collection through the courts. (Rose 1986; NV Senate Bill 335 [1985])

The role of silent observer remains an important one for government today. It was incorporated in the Indian Gaming Regulatory Act, passed by Congress in 1988. The law allows self-regulation by tribes on traditional Indian games, such as wagers on athletic contests. Another provision stipulates National Indian Gaming Commission regulation of bingo for two years, after which a tribe can be certified for self-regulation (if, of course, all goes well during the preceding two years). Casino game regulation, on the other hand, was placed in the joint domain of states and tribes.

Most charity gaming in America remains self-regulated by operators, and the level of oversight for some forms of commercial gaming is limited to traditional law enforcement functions.

Minor Government Regulation

A third governmental role may involve legalized private gambling with minimal standards and regulatory procedures. For instance, operators may be required to have a permit and agree to certain rules, such as hours of operation and wager limits. Operators also may be required to file reports of their activities. Regulation of charitable bingo games and raffles often falls into this minimal level of activity—that is, when there is any regulation required at all.

The regulation of slot machine gaming follows this pattern in some states where lotteries place the machines (called video lottery terminals, or VLTs) in private establishments. Computerized data systems account for the cash flow through the machines, but there usually is little additional oversight. VLT programs are advanced in the sense that they bring healthy revenues to governments and private entrepreneurs without the necessity of bureaucratic agencies to control them. The system of lottery ticket distribution is quite similar.

In Nevada, as detailed below, there is a well-developed system of government control over casinos. But the relatively small number of regulators focuses nearly all their attention on the larger casinos of Las Vegas, Reno, Lake Tahoe, and Laughlin. Establishments in these towns hold hundreds or even thousands of slot machines, and scores of gaming tables. Regulators find themselves with little time for policing the nearly 2000 restricted holders that operate 15 or fewer slot machines. Since these licensees pay fixed taxes on each machine, there is no need for the government to track cash flow, and the state's main concern is that the machines are manufactured by companies that can assure properly functioning mechanisms.

Specialized Government Regulation

A fourth role of government is to administer detailed regulatory processes through special boards and commissions. These processes include the licensing of operators and employees, preceded by extensive background investigations; establishing the precise rules for each game played; careful ongoing monitoring of gaming activities with on-premise inspections by board or commission employees; detailed accounting of financial transactions involved in the gaming operations; and the collection of fees and specific taxes. North American governments which permit commercial casino gambling and wagering on horse and dog races typically follow this pattern of extensive regulation by specialized administrative units.

The philosophy of regulation can vary considerably in these situations. Nevada emphasizes control through internal casino management. The legislature has created a two-tiered structure with the full-time Gaming Control Board and the part-time Nevada Gaming Commission. The board conducts thorough background investigations on all license applicants and makes license recommendations to the commission. The commission makes the final decision on the application. (Cabot and Rubenstein 1993)

The Nevada Gaming Commission does not maintain a staff. The Gaming Control Board staff, consisting of fewer than 100 field inspectors, is responsible for visits to well over 2,000 gaming sites, including the major casinos plus all businesses offering slot machines only. A staff of board auditors monitors independent audits conducted for the casinos by accounting firms. This staff is large enough to conduct only a very few on-sight spot audits. A tax division of the board collects gaming taxes and fees and transfers these to the state treasury. Except for application investigation fees, which are paid by the casinos, all regulatory costs incurred are financed out of the general state budget, as authorized by legislative appropriations.

The state also has provisions for a Gaming Policy Committee, which may offer advice to the legislature and to the commission regarding casino laws and regulations. However, this committee has rarely been called by the governor to meet. (Gaming Control Board 1977)

New Jersey offers a contrasting model of casino regulation. A five-member Casino Control Commission, appointed by the governor, works beside the Division of Gaming Enforcement within the state Attorney General's office. These two entities have large staffs and share functions. The division is responsible for investigating all license applications, reviewing casino operations with inspections and audits of books, and prosecuting regulatory violations in front of the commission. The division also makes license recommendations to the commission, which may conduct independent investigations before making final decisions. The commission is empowered to police casino operations. Members of its staff are present in casinos at all times that gaming is being conducted. The commission also collects casino fees and taxes, assigns the costs of regulation to individual casinos, and collects these expenses as well. (Lehne 1986) Either the commission or the division may initiate investigations into gaming conduct at any time.

While Nevada requires licenses only for establishments, owners, and key employees, New Jersey requires them for each employee. The more intense, hands-on regulatory approach taken by New Jersey has come about because most New Jersey casinos began operations at about the same time (within three or four years of one another) within an atmosphere of suspicion and concern about organized crime. The contrasting approaches of the two states are reflected in regulation costs. In one year the New Jersey Commission and Division of Gaming Enforcement spent over $80 million to regulate 12 casinos in one city. Nevada's Gaming Control Board and Commission spent $18 million to regulate 351 unrestricted casinos (offering both slot machines and table games) and nearly 2,000 restricted casinos (15 or fewer slot machines) statewide.

Horse-racing operations also require close supervision and regulation. Almost all jurisdictions that allow such wagering have specialized racing commissions. These commissions approve applications of the "associations" that are created by track owners to organize betting. The commissioners also assign dates for races and collect license fees and revenues from betting pools. Commission staffs conduct financial audits and appoint stewards to oversee the integrity of the races. Horses are tested to assure that no illegal drugs influence the outcome of races. (Day 1950)

Racing commissioners also rely upon other organizations to assist in track regulation. A National Association of State Racing Commissioners helps standardize rules among the states, and exchanges information on racing participants. The American Jockey Club is a private organization of horse owners and others who are interested in the breeding industry. The club publishes a detailed book called the *Rules of Racing* which is sanctioned by the commissions. The Jockey Club also manages what is called the *Stud Book*. This is a registry of all thoroughbreds eligible to run in horse races. The club and the track associations appoint stewards who, along with the state commission's stewards, monitor all races. (Day 1950)

Government as Entrepreneur

A fifth role of government is that of entrepreneur. Governments own gambling operations and manage them as if they were private enterprises. The lotteries in 37 states and 10 provinces are all entrepreneurial government operations. Canadian provinces also run casinos. For instance, the Crystal Casino in Winnipeg is operated by the Manitoba Lottery Corporation, a branch of the Manitoba Government's Ministry of Finance. The corporation runs bingo halls and a slot machine system throughout the province. Seven other provinces and states run networks of video lottery terminals through their lottery organizations.

The fact that gambling operations are actually run by governments has done much to allay public fears that games are dishonest or controlled by organized crime. Lotteries are considered a "clean," even "proper," means of collecting public revenues. Moreover, critics of gambling believe it is important to have direct public oversight for gambling to assure that operations meet public standards for propriety. As long as gambling operators themselves are public employees, this oversight control can remain strong.

Yet there are strong opponents to government-operated gambling. These detractors claim that government should not encourage gambling or, for that matter, any other commercial activity. As gaming operators, governments must eventually encourage participation in the activity and there is potential for conflicts of interest and dishonesty. Cheating does occur in government casinos, and lottery operations have been compromised. Does government have the innate ability to close down its own tarnished revenue generators as it does to close dishonest private gambling enterprises? Probably not.

Many gambling operations require large initial capital investments. Governments could find themselves at considerable risk by entering such ventures. Also, governments may be reluctant to invest the capital necessary to make operations viable. In the same light, governments that operate with civil service pay schedules may be hesitant to offer gaming executive salaries comparable to those earned by executives in the private sector. Hence, government may lose access to the best talent.

A final concern about government-sponsored gaming is the impact it has on law enforcement. Efforts to control illegal gambling can be weakened if citizens, police, prosecutors, and judges surrender to predispositions of government-generated "cleanliness." Indeed, defendants charged with illegal gaming may assert that their only crime is that they are engaged in competition with a government monopoly.

Why Do People Gamble?

People have asked this question for centuries. Answers to the question have invariably been the same. Gamblers are deviants and people who gamble violate the rules of government, society, and religion. Gamblers are possessed of criminal minds or are in some other way depraved or subject to evil spirits.

While considerable scholarly attention is still given to the psychological and personality disorders of certain kinds of gamblers (usually pathological or compulsive), the notion that gambling is in and of itself deviant is now clearly rejected.

How can gambling be considered somehow abnormal when overwhelming numbers of adults engage in it? A 1975 study by the University of Michigan Survey Research Center revealed that 61 percent of the participants had participated in gambling during the previous year. More than 80 percent indicated they approved of legalizing some form of gambling activity. (Commission on the Review 1976) Atlantic City casinos attract over 30 million visitors each year, while Las Vegas welcomes 23 million. These gamblers come from all sectors of the population. They are male and female, rich and poor, Protestant, Catholic, and Jewish. They represent all races and educational levels. The gambling industry is expanding as more and more normal, responsible, rational human beings engage in gambling.

Since life is full of risks, the risks associated with gambling can also be viewed as elements of a "regular" existence. It has been so since the beginning of time, with every known society gambling in one form or another. Many reasons can be used to explain why normal people gamble. Some of them are rational; others are almost completely void of rationality.

Some people actually treat gambling as an investment. For them, gambling is a calculated technique for making money. These people are professional gamblers. (Dombrink and Thompson 1990) The professional gambler seeks to discover ways to beat the odds—it is possible. Professionals at horse tracks carefully study the performance of horses and jockeys and examine the running times for various distances under various weather conditions at different times of the year. Armed with such information, these gamblers may actually gain an edge over the posted odds. Similarly, sports gamblers closely follow baseball, basketball, and football teams. They collect information regarding players' injuries, coaching styles, and performance trends in home or away games.

Professional poker players endeavor to cultivate betting and bluffing skills to their advantage. Proficiency with these skills, or a lack thereof, can indeed, make "every hand a winner" or "every hand a loser," as Kenny Rogers sings in his popular song, "The

Gambler." Poker requires an intimate knowledge of card distribution and probability, but the true skill in poker comes in the ability to read other people. Professionals hone these skills through years of experience. While the odds are fixed against every player in games like craps and roulette, players compete against one another in poker—a contest where one player *has* to win.

Other professional gamblers are drawn to progressive jackpot games. Such jackpots are found with some casino slot machines or with government lottery games known as *lotto*. In lotto and at progressive slot machines a portion of a player's loss is put into a jackpot each time the player loses. The jackpot thus grows until one player wins. When the jackpot reaches a certain amount, the odds actually begin to favor all the players. The odds of winning a million dollar jackpot, for instance, may be two million to one. However, because of previous player losses, the jackpot may have increased to $3 million while the odds remain at two million to one. Logically and rationally, the chances for "good" bets have increased.

Sometimes, gangs of professional gamblers will virtually monopolize a casino floor, pulling handles on all the machines tied into the progressive jackpot. These teams will play the slots for hours—even days—until one of them wins the big jackpot. Recently a group of Australian businessmen noticed that the lotto jackpot in the state of Virginia had reached a level where it was a very good gamble. They set out to purchase tickets with every possible combination of numbers, investing millions in their wager—and they won. This group did benefit from a bit of luck. Had an unassociated player selected the same winning number, the prize would have been divided in two and the group would have come out on the losing end. But the ploy worked, proving that gambling can be a very good financial "investment." (*New York Times* 25 February 1992; *New York Times* 28 February 1992)

Sometimes it may be economically rational to gamble when the odds are stacked clearly against a player. Consider the value of one dollar to a poor person. Can this dollar bill carry very much value at any specific point in time? A dollar cannot buy many groceries. It can't pay all the rent or purchase clothing or otherwise wield very much power to improve the quality of life in any discernible or lasting fashion. The loss of that dollar, therefore, would not be considered a major setback, or even a noticeable event. But while a dollar means very little in these times, it still buys a poor person the chance to win $10,000 or $1 million or $100 million in a lottery. Any such prize would be a godsend for a poor person. Hence, some gambles, while not likely to bring the big prize, represent an exchange of something with little value for something else that, potentially, can be of a very high value. The specific odds in this case are quite irrelevant to the logic of placing the bet.

While the poor usually lose in such games, lottery tickets give them dreams and hopes for a better existence. Some of these people may actually realize these dreams. Or they may win smaller prizes that can bring moments or short periods of great happiness. Gordon Moody is a Methodist minister and founder of the Moody House for problem gamblers in London. This author had occasion to speak with him about the English lottery. While a criticism of the government-sponsored game was expected, Moody surprisingly referred to the lottery as "a bit of kindness" for the working class poor. The lottery, he said, allowed poor people to dream of someday having an automobile or a better apartment. "What other chance do they have?" Moody asked. (Moody 1990)

For the middle class and the affluent, gambling can offer benefits not measurable in financial terms. Most gambling takes place in a social setting, usually outside the home, and therefore represents an opportunity to spend time with friends. This social benefit represents perhaps the greatest motivation for bingo players. Similarly, casino gaming is a popular recreation, taking place as it does in crowded, party-like settings; but even lotteries played in complete isolation can have social benefits. The drawing of a winning number is a shared experience. The very thought of the prize stimulates optimists to seek one another out to share dreams and plans. The game also contributes to community dialogue, which might otherwise be limited to the weather, or last night's newscast. Indeed, a survey of California lottery players found that having fun was the reason half of them had purchased tickets.

Some players justify their gambling habits as a method of contributing to charity. Many bingo operations appeal to these kinds of sentiments, as do lotteries, which often market the game as an elemental financial component of some educational program, park project, or other noble cause.

The horse-betting parlor is perhaps one of the most socially oriented institutions in the gambling world. For participants, the parlor becomes an attractive alternative to the monotony and boredom of their "regular" lives. In this escapist world, the gambler assumes new roles for brief moments or hours. No longer a father, husband, worker, or supervisor, he is stripped of outside social standing. New social standings are assigned to those players who win races, or those who have valuable information on the next race. It is very much a temporary world—one that allows people to forget the conditions and problems of life. (Rosecrance 1988)

Las Vegas operates on the notion that people need such an escape—a three- or seven-day vacation where they can forget their tensions, regenerate their spirits, and forget business deals or other concerns. In gambling, the only deals that matter are the ones struck with cards or dice, and even though gambling can be very stimulating, it has a soothing effect on players. However, the excitement of the activity can be just as prevalent as the relaxation it brings, and the excitement of gambling is, in fact, usually given more emphasis in advertising. Gambling brings a psychological rush. It focuses the attention and makes the blood flow a little faster.

Gambling can also give some players a fleeting illusion of self-control. This is valuable to those whose lives are manipulated and programmed by forces beyond their influence. Whether the person is selecting a number for a lottery ticket or a number on a roulette wheel, the cognizance of making that choice independently is satisfying. The gambler can choose whether to play or not, how much to wager, which number to select, or which strategy to pursue.

Some players carry this illusion of control a step further. They feel they have a special mystique that allows them to beat the odds. Most of these personality types never contemplate the true mathematical odds, which do not favor them, and certainly the lotteries and casinos do not openly inform gamblers of their disadvantage. Still, for brief moments in the gambling world delusions of self-control can offset the realities of a grimmer life, which more often than not is controlled by others.

The author's study of Latin American casinos reveals that male players use gambling as an arena for demonstrating machismo. Since Latin American society denies most men the perception that they are dominant or in charge, gambling becomes an outlet for assertiveness. When the gambler wins, he can strut to the admiration of others, who may start to place their own bets and demonstrate their own bravado. (Thompson 1991)

Professor Felicia Florine Campbell suggests that gambling should be available to seniors in rest homes because so many of the elderly are trapped in boring, lonely routines dedicated almost entirely to physical preservation. She argues that the presence of slot machines would give residents something to look forward to or dream about, and gambling could increase the motivation of the elderly.

In recent years, several large casinos catering to seniors have been established in Las Vegas, including Sam's Town, the Gold Coast, Arizona Charlie's, and the Santa Fe. These casinos provide buses to transport seniors to and from the gambling halls. As one walks through these establishments he must keep an eye out for aged players in wheelchairs or with walkers or oxygen tanks. Indeed, even though slot machines do not exist in nursing homes, many seniors still do enjoy gambling excitement in casinos. (Campbell 1974)

Critics of this marketing thrust toward elderly gamblers finger casino owners as crass profiteers who are taking advantage of senior citizens' desperation, boredom, and loneliness. Gambling, in fact, affects the psychological weaknesses of many kinds of players— especially those who have little control over their wagering habits. These people can lose the ability to manage their finances while gambling, and in turn, the ability to support their families. In some cases they may turn to violent loan agents (loan sharks) or resort to criminal activities to fund their habit. This kind of activity can take them further and further down the road of self-destruction. At the extreme, some gamblers have even committed suicide.

While there are many positive and even logical reasons for being a gambler, some compulsive players do lose sight of rationality. Estimates of the number of compulsive players in the gambling crowd range from 1 to 5 percent. Why do these people gamble so relentlessly? Explanations have drawn on Freudian personality analyses, learned behavior and reinforcement theory, and social experience models of behavior. We examine these explanations below.

Social and Religious Views of Gaming

Social Views

Three major surveys on gambling were conducted in 1974, 1982, and 1992. The Survey Research Center of the University of Michigan conducted one of them for a national commission on gambling policy in 1974. It found that 61 percent of the population had gambled during the previous year. (Commission on the Review 1976) Males were found to gamble more than females, whites more than non-whites, highly educated players more than less-educated ones, and younger people more than older people. In addition, Catholics were identified as more likely to gamble than Protestants, Jews, Methodists, Baptists, and Fundamentalists.

A majority of the respondents favored bingo legalization (68 percent), horse betting (62 percent), and lotteries (61 percent). Less than half supported legalization of dog betting (49 percent), casinos (40 percent), and off-track betting (38 percent), while less than one third approved legalized sports betting (32 percent).

The second survey was commissioned by *Gaming Business Magazine* and conducted by the Gallup organization in August 1982. (Klein and Selsner 1982) During the eight intervening years between these two studies, casinos were authorized and opened in Atlantic City and new lotteries were established in several states. In the second survey, a majority supported the legalization of most forms of gambling: bingo (74 percent), lotteries (72 percent), off-track betting (54 percent), and casinos in resort areas (51 percent). Only the legalization of betting on professional sporting events failed to win majority support (48 percent approving). In contrast to the 61 percent that indicated they gambled in the first survey, only 40 percent of the Gallup respondents said they had gambled during the previous year.

Another national poll sponsored by the Harrah's casino organization in 1992 found that 50 percent of the adult population had visited a casino at some time; 22 percent had made visits during the previous year. Respondents indicated entertainment as their primary motivation for gambling. Higher proportions of gamblers were found in the northeastern and western states than in the midwestern or southern states. Harrah's also pinpointed a solid majority of Americans—55 percent—who supported the view that gambling was "perfectly acceptable for anyone." Thirty-five percent indicated that gambling was "acceptable for others, but not for me." Only 10 percent said gambling should not be acceptable for anyone.

Actual election returns indicate that voters are indeed becoming more permissive. Public lottery propositions are nearly always winning approval, and support for other forms of gambling, while mixed, is increasing. Prior to 1988 (with the exception of a 1976 New Jersey vote) all campaigns for casinos failed, but since South

Dakota approved limited casino gaming for the town of Dead-wood in 1988, successful campaigns for casinos have been waged in Colorado (1990) and Missouri (1992).

Public support for gaming is also evidenced in the increasing numbers of legislative endorsements of gambling. Casinos have been accepted by legislatures in Iowa (1989), Illinois (1990), Mississippi (1991), Louisiana (1992), and Indiana (1993). The provincial governments of Ontario, Quebec, and Manitoba have also approved casino gaming. While these propositions have normally incorporated gaming limitations of some kind (numbers of games, the size of bets, numbers and locations of casinos), they do illustrate a new public willingness to embrace gambling.

As the uninitiated receive more exposure to gambling near their hometowns, they may cast off old inhibitions and sample the activity themselves. If they find gambling to be entertaining, positive attitudes and permissiveness may grow even more. The surveys cited above have found greater acceptance of gaming in regions where there is more of it, specifically the Northeast and the West.

Elections and legislative campaigns reveal more than just the popular view of gambling. Political maneuvering and lobbying is orchestrated by powerful interests with considerable financial resources. Many campaigns for casinos and lotteries are well-supported by gaming industry companies, while opposition groups often tend to coalesce around church organizations and ad hoc civic groups that have limited funding.

Church interests spent $22,000 in an effort to defeat casinos in New Jersey in 1976, while casino supporters spent over $1.3 million to turn votes in their favor. A single company, Resorts International, contributed the largest share of funding—over $200,000. This helped the firm win the state's first casino licenses and windfall profits that exceeded $100 million before a second casino was licensed to compete with them. Likewise, Colorado casino supporters outspent their opponents nearly 75 to 1. Many of the proponents were able to cash in on their campaign investments by either winning licenses for casinos or selling land to casino developers. (Dombrink and Thompson 1990)

The campaign for a California lottery was supported by a $2 million donation from a supply company that subsequently won a $40 million contract to furnish instant lottery tickets. This contribution certainly turned out to be a good business investment. Conversely, churches and civic organizations can achieve moral victories, but are not likely to reap financial rewards if they are successful in halting gambling propositions. It certainly is not realistic for them to expect more plate donations, as their appeals for campaign money have probably exhausted their parishioners' and constituents' resources.

Money and the expectation of financial reward drives gambling movements. In the process, the public can find itself a pawn, or even a passive partner. People may not want gambling, but they may discover that they desire additional tax burdens even less. Gambling, when presented in a positive light with unchallenged advertisements, can be sold as the lesser of the two evils — consequently winning public approval.

Religious Views

Patterns of public attitude toward gambling also have religious dimensions. The 1974 University of Michigan survey suggested that gambling was legal in some states and not in others because of religious dynamics. Personal attitudes on gambling are no doubt formed to a certain degree by religious principles.

Since the dawn of civilization and the most rudimentary emergence of religion, the pious have been concerned with gambling. While the activity has been recognized dogmatically as a sin, religious organizations nevertheless tend to incorporate gambling into their agendas. Only a small part of the religious community advocates a wholesale condemnation of gambling and most faiths take the view that the activity is not harmful with proper control and moderation.

There have been many rationales for religious censure of gambling. Some doctrines maintain that individuals should seek purity and perfection as a ticket to salvation and heaven. These religions view gambling as a sin that detours the participant from the path of cleanliness and righteousness. This view holds that gambling unearths wanton feelings, a desire for worldly goods, and inattentiveness to the work ethic. The religious may feel that gambling destroys a person's sense of responsibility or his ability to care for and support loved ones. They assert that gambling diverts one's personal attentions from God and consumes time that could be spent in serious contemplation of prayer and ritual.

Religious doctrine also morally condemns gambling as a form of stealing. Gambling winners, church leaders argue, gain property from gambling losers without giving back something valuable in exchange. The gambler is viewed as disrespectful to the material domain of others and to the prerogatives of God. Some faiths may reason that personal property ownership does not actually exist because, in truth, all belongs to God. Mortals are thought to be only leasing pieces of a deity's estate—and one clause in that lease is that mortals be good stewards of the property. Gambling, these religions submit, is not a responsible method of house-sitting in God's world. In such a moralistic context, a religion may view people who engage in wagering as literal thieves.

Church elders say that by participating in gambling, we trifle with God's plan for the universe. These doctrines assert that fortune is the sole prerogative of God. Gambling denigrates God's options and scoffs at His control over our destiny. Several variations of such religious themes arise in different religious organizations. We can also find discussions of gambling in the mythologies and rituals of many faiths. These passages depict battles between God and Satan as the chief determinants of the fate of gambling.

Still, many religious organizations approve of gambling, most notably the lottery form, and proceeds from these games are usually earmarked for more traditional church purposes.

Biblical References

A majority of Americans are tied through family and culture to faiths of Judeo-Christian origin. It may be instructive to examine biblical references of these faiths to gambling.

While there are no explicit condemnations of gambling, even in the Ten Commandments, the following passage from Isaiah in the Old Testament (65:11–12) comes very close: "But you who forsake the Lord ... who set a table for fortune and fill cups of mixed wine for destiny, I will destine you to the sword, and all of you shall bow down to the slaughter."

In Proverbs (13:11) it is suggested that winnings from gambling activity are ephemeral: "Wealth hastily gotten will dwindle, but he who gathers little by little will increase it." Other scriptures suggest that gambling may be wrong because it represents covertness or stealing, which is directly condemned (Exodus 20:15, 17).

Many biblical passages that refer to gambling-like activities defer judgment. Rather, they are impartial acknowledgment of the use of lotteries for various purposes. The Old Testament view of the lottery was often considered to derive directly from the word of God. High priests used a lottery technique called Urim and Tummin to make decisions (Exodus 28:30; Leviticus 8:7–9). Sailors turned to the drawing of lots to determine who among them had sinned and caused inclement weather. In one familiar biblical story, the results pointed to Jonah, who was cast overboard (Jonah 1:7–8). Saul was chosen by drawing to be king (1 Samuel 10:20–21), and David was instructed in a drawing which way to go to take command of his troops (2 Samuel 2:1). Soldiers were selected for battle by lottery (Judges 20:9) and lotteries were used to divide lands, select the first residents of Jerusalem (Nehemiah 11:1), and select animals for sacrifice on the day of atonement (Leviticus 16:7–10).

The New Testament contains additional lottery references. For instance, a twelfth disciple (Mathais) was selected to replace Judas by means of a drawing (Acts 1:21–26). Another notable story refers to the Roman Centurions who rolled dice for the robes of Christ at the crucifixion (Matthew 27:35). This is one of the rare cases where gambling is presented in the Bible as a means for selfish gain, and in this context, the activity has to be considered very negative. In all other Biblical references, lotteries are used for serious purposes rather than for games.

Christian

With the mixed body of biblical evidence, some Judeo-Christian denominations categorically repudiate all gambling, while others adopt the opposite view—that gambling in and of itself is not sinful. These views are connected to two general schools of ethics: the teleological or worldly view, and the deontological or universal view.

Teleological ethics seeks to examine a particular activity and asks whether the activity results in positive or negative results. This system of thought has parallels in the notions of positive law, and subscribes to the notion that it is the prerogative of humans to understand when an activity is right or wrong, beneficial or harmful, and when to regulate it. In recent years, the term "situational ethics" has become attached to the teleological perspective. Certain fundamentalist groups term the teleological approach one of "secular humanism". Those who hold to this viewpoint regard some gambling as permissible and some as sinful, depending on its context.

The deontological or universal system of ethics maintains that gambling and other "sinful" activity is wrong at all times and under all conditions. This system has parallels in natural law, or the law that is thought to be God-given, absolute, and eternal.

Churches need not be consistent on their treatment of sin. Religious doctrine, whatever its ultimate source, is interpreted and translated by many over the centuries. Consistency is difficult for the individual, no less entire groups, no matter how divinely inspired they believe their position to be. Catholic doctrine has a decidedly natural law and deontological orientation, but on the issue of gambling the Catholic Church falls very much into the teleological camp. This is not to suggest that Catholics fail to recognize problems in gambling behavior. L. M. Starkey writes in *Money, Mania, and Morals* that "Catholic moralists are agreed that gambling and betting may lead to grave abuse and sin, especially when they are prompted by mere gain. The gambler usually frequents bad company, wastes much valuable time, becomes adverse to work, is strongly tempted to be dishonest when luck is against him, and often brings financial ruin upon himself and those dependent upon him." (Starkey 1964)

The argument is not complete without consideration of the issue of freedom. As *The New Catholic Encyclopedia* states, "A person is entitled to dispose of his own property as he wills . . . so long as in doing so he does not render himself incapable of fulfilling duties incumbent upon him by reason of justice or charity. Gambling, therefore, though a luxury, is not considered sinful except when the indulgence in it is inconsistent with duty." (*The New Catholic Encyclopedia* 1967)

Catholic Church doctrine considers as sinful that person who gambles with someone else's money, or with money needed for the support of others. The church also condemns gambling when it becomes compulsive or disruptive to family and social relationships. Moreover, the freedom to gamble implies a knowing freedom to enter into a fair and honest contract for play. Cheating at gambling is considered wrong, as are all dishonest games.

The church also judges gambling according its consequences. When results are favorable, gambling may be viewed as worthy of promotion. An example of this is the limited stakes bingo games that are conducted inside the church for purposes of raising funds for schools or hospitals.

When considering their position on gambling legalization, church leaders want to know if the activity places disadvantages on poor people, results in pathological behavior, or is monitored to ensure honesty. Since the status of these criteria vary from situation to situation, the church has supported some public referenda while opposing others.

The Church of England and its offspring, the American Episcopal Church (essentially reformed Catholic organizations) both accept the Catholic approach toward gambling.

Most Protestant denominations, as well as Baptists, Mormons, and Jehovah's Witnesses, categorically oppose gambling as a sinful recreation. This deontological or absolute ethical perspective is reflected in many official church statements. The Social Principles of the United Methodist Church proclaims that

> Gambling is a menace to society, deadly to the best interests of moral, social, economic, and spiritual life, and destructive of good government. As an act of faith and love, Christians should abstain from gambling and should strive to minister to those victimized by the practice. . . . Community standards and personal lifestyles should be such as would make unnecessary and undesirable the resort to commercial gambling, including public lotteries, as a recreation, as an escape, or as a means of producing public revenue or funds for support of charities or government. (General Conference of United Methodist Church 1984)

The Southern Baptist Convention is the largest non-Catholic denomination in America. Their Director of Family and Moral Concerns told the Commission on the Review of the National Policy on Gambling much the same story:

> In all its resolutions, the Southern Baptist Convention has rejected gambling. Obviously, some forms of gambling are more serious than others, but all forms have been consistently rejected in Southern Baptist statements and resolutions. . . . The use of gambling profits for worthy activities has not led Southern Baptists to endorse gambling. . . . The availability of gambling tempts both the reformed gambler and the potential gambler to destruction. For the entire community, gambling is disruptive and harmful. Thus, concerned citizens should work for laws to control and eliminate gambling. (Bell 1976)

The Salvation Army opposes gambling, and the Church of Jesus Christ of Latter Day Saints (Mormons) has been vehement in maintaining its disapproval. In 1926, church President Heber J. Grant proclaimed, "The Church has been and now is unalterably opposed to gambling in any form whatever. [A]ll members of the Church [are urged] to refrain from participation in any games of chance or risky speculation." (Grant 1926)

An interesting side issue arose in the Mormon Church recently over temple privileges. Mormon church members must be in good standing in order to enter temples, but Mormons who work in gambling establishments or in gambling-related jobs can be denied entry. When the church decided to build a temple in Las Vegas (about 10 percent of the Las Vegas population are Mormons) the number of members holding jobs in casinos prompted a review of policy. Church leaders decided that casino workers who did not personally gamble and did not overtly encourage others to do so would retain good standing status as long as they met other church obligations.

Jewish

Religious principles in the Jewish faith are interpreted and applied through tenets derived from Jewish scripture and other religious works, such as the Torah. Rabbis, or religious scholars, are trained to interpret the religious law, much as Supreme Court judges are trained to interpret constitutional law.

Jewish law has changed and grown over time, and is subject to a variety of interpretations, so rabbinical scholars have offered many interpretations of gambling throughout history. Today there is no singular Jewish view of gambling, but there is a trend toward the teleological orientation. Jews certainly do not universally condemn gambling, but the constant state of disagreement that exists in Jewish intellectual circles ensures a plethora of opinions. One legal interpretation, for example, disqualified two types of gamblers—dice players and pigeon racers—from standing as witnesses in court. A rabbi maintained that these gamblers were committing theft by accepting winnings, but another scholar disputed this, arguing that only the habitual gamblers should be disqualified, and the disqualification should derive not from the indictment of gamblers as thieves, but rather because the activity does not further the "betterment of society." (Jacobs 1973)

Another rabbi said it is permissible to participate in gambling when the "stakes are placed on the table," but never in games where players incur debt. Jewish moralists have endorsed lotteries as acceptable so long as lottery winners realize their good fortunes are a blessing from God. Other Jewish communities, however, disdain the "get-rich-quick" attitude connected with lottery playing and prohibit participation, even while admitting that ancient Jewish law doesn't forbid gambling. These thinkers view gambling as a route to financial ruin and family deterioration. (Jacobs 1973)

Political groups within the Jewish faith have issued aggressive denunciations of gambling. A resolution of the Central Conference of American Rabbis called upon its members to discourage their congregations from using gambling for fund raising. The group said the use of lotteries, off-track betting, or any other form of gambling promoted by government agencies to raise revenues is deplorable, and called upon fellow Jews "to provide counsel for compulsive gamblers and their families." (Resolution of Central Conference of American Rabbis, 97th Annual Convention, Snowmass, Colorado, June 26–July 1, 1986)

The United Synagogue of America has vigorously opposed the legalization of bingo games for charitable purposes. They have held that raising money for religious purposes is in and of itself a religious activity which must not be defiled by gambling. In 1960 a Brooklyn, New York, congregation was expelled from the association of synagogues for allowing bingo games to be used for religious fund raising. (Starkly 1964)

These contemporary views seem to belie Jewish history. Gambling has long been part of Jewish tradition and culture and is often tied to religious celebrations. On the holiest Jewish holiday of Yom Kippur, one story relates, Aaron took two goats to the temple. There, one of them was selected by lottery to be sacrificed to atone for the sins of the Jewish people. The other goat was sent off to the wilderness. Then there is the ritual of Urim and Tummin, used by high priests to assist in making decisions. In this practice, two small stones were wrapped with papers on which different decisions to a question were recorded. One of the stones would then be randomly drawn from the priest's breastplate.

About 2,500 years ago, a Persian king arranged to massacre the Jewish people and selected the day for the attack with a roll of dice. However, the day chosen turned out to be a bad day for such a campaign and the Jewish people escaped. The dice apparently had favored them, and a Jewish holiday known as Purim was established to celebrate the lucky day with merrymaking and gambling. Hanukkah, too, is seen as a "lucky" day because of its connection to the story of Jewish survival with the assistance of a single oil lamp. A theme of Hanukkah is that faith can bring much from little. Thus, the lamp celebration is held on Hanukkah, which is also known as "the New Year's Day for Gamblers." (Linn 1986)

Notwithstanding the many indulgences in gambling on these holidays, Jewish law and Jewish authorities still frown on the practice. Throughout history Jewish leaders have regarded the professional gambler as an outcast—"he is a thief . . . and plays no part in the betterment of society." (Jacobs 1973) The gambler is "untrustworthy" and "wastes time in idleness." It has been thought that time spent gambling is lost from study and productivity. (Werblowsky and Wigoder 1966)

At times, these scholars have even interpreted disasters such as storms and pestilence as punishment for gambling. Accordingly, gambling has been banned, save for the above-mentioned holidays. Even then, gambling gets a nod of approval only if players do not participate for selfish gain. Winning players are expected to donate moneys to charity. (Linn 1986)

Islamic

In the year 610, a story goes, the Prophet Muhammad was approached by an angel who revealed to him the Word of God. The Word of God was transcribed as the Koran, Islam's most holy book. Muhammad spent the next 22 years of his life traveling and teaching the Word. The Word prescribed the methods of living a holy life, and Muhammad directed his own actions accordingly. His life and the Koran serve as benchmarks for a faith now followed by nearly a billion people in North Africa, the Middle East, and Asia.

The Koran and Islam take a very negative view toward gambling. The following passages are found in the Koran:

> They will ask you about wine and maysir [a gambling game]: In both is a great sin as well as some uses for people. The sin is greater than their usefulness. (Sura 2:219)

> Only would Satan sow hatred and strife among you, by wine and games of chance, and turn you aside from the remembrance of God, and from prayer; will ye not, therefore, abstain from them? (Sura 5:90–93)

Islam regards gambling as "unjustified enrichment," and the process of "receiving a monetary advantage without giving a countervalue." Evidence presented by gamblers is not admissible in an Islamic court, and anyone in the faith that receives gambling proceeds is obligated to donate them to the poor. Gambling is generally placed in the category of amusement, and Islamic jurists have ruled that "every amusement is worthless frivolity if it distracts from obedience to God." (Rosenthal 1975) If a person allowed the "time for prayer to pass without praying, because he is engrossed in the game . . . it indicates disrespect for his duties." (Rosenthal 1975)

There are a few exceptions in the Islamic religion to the prohibition on gambling. Wagering is permitted for horse racing because such betting was historically an incentive for military training. By participating in racing, the faithful Islamic maintained not only his fitness but the readiness of his steed so that both could answer when called to fight infidels in the holy wars. Similarly, betting was permitted on shooting contests, and prizes could be given for winners of competitions involving Islamic law and religion. Such prizes, even if given in the context of wagering, provided additional incentives for the adherents of Islam to be worthy and faithful. (Schacht 1964)

Hindu

The philosophy and ethics practiced by Hindus dominate much of India and the subcontinent of South Asia—a region populated by a billion people. Hinduism is the oldest living religion and is quite dynamic, growing more with the new teachings of Hindu masters and gurus. Hindus worship a litany of gods, often in the form of physical statues or idols, and acknowledge them for various purposes. The religion has no single founder, no central organization, and no leader. It also has no single book of doctrine. Rather, a series of books conveys interpretations of what the Hindu gods demand, and collectively espouses a few central precepts. Moral beliefs are referred to as the dharma of Hinduism.

One basic Hindu conviction is that people must renounce the world and withdraw in order to obtain liberation. Different people can choose different paths to reach liberation. Hinduism is a religion which espouses that liberation and death can lead to rebirth in a higher class or social status. Eventually, the faith holds, righteous believers can ascend to a godlike status and achieve Nirvana. However, those who are bad or who lead worldly lives without seeking liberation are punished with reincarnation in lower social class or life form—even that of an animal.

The dharma of Hinduism as expressed in Hindu books contains many references to gambling. The mythology of the faith discusses the gambling play of Hindu gods which, when speaking to Hindu mortals, admonish against gambling. In the early Vedic era, epic poems were recorded in the *Rig Veda*. One was called the

"Hymn of the Gambler," or "The Gamester's Lament." In it, the
God Savitr warns against gambling:

> She did not scold me, or lose her temper
> She was kind to my friends and me
> But because of a throw two high by one
> I have rejected my loving wife. . . .
>
> Her mother hates me; my wife repels me
> A man in trouble finds no one to pity him
> They say, "I've no more use for a gambler
> than for a worn-out horse put up for sale. . . ."
>
> The dice are armed with hooks and piercing,
> they are deceptive, hot and burning, like children
> they give and take again, they strike back at
> their conquerors. They are sweetened with honey through
> the magic they work on the gambler. . . .
>
> The gambler grieves when he sees a woman,
> another man's wife, in their pleasant home.
> In the morning he yokes the chestnut horses [dice]
> In the evening he falls by the hearth, a beggar
>
> Don't play with dice, but plough your furrow!
> Delight in your property, prize it highly!
> Look to your cattle and look to your wife,
> you gambler! Thus noble Savitr tells me.

Source: Bashman, A.L. *The Wonder That Was India*. Calcutta: Rupa
Company, 1967.

Since knowledge was regarded as one of the paths toward
liberation, Hindu students received special treatment in the law.
They were also warned not to gamble, and indoctrinated with the
belief that those who do gamble will die young and "go to Hell"—
an uncomfortable purgatory-like existence—while awaiting rebirth in a more miserable condition. (Hopkins 1924) Hinduism
lifts this prohibition for adults, but disallows cheating. Adults are
allowed to enter the historic gambling halls of kings, who were
warned, but allowed to gamble. The *Laws of Manu* advises kings
that gambling is one of the most "pernicious" of the royal vices.
(*Encyclopedia of Religion* 1928) The divine Krishna added that gambling was the worst "desire-born" vice.

In the Vedic era, repentant gamblers sought out heavenly
nymphs, who themselves gambled, and begged forgiveness. (Hopkins 1924)

Under Hindu law, gamblers are disqualified as legal witnesses, and due to their "depravity" are considered "thieves and assassins"—people in whom "no truth can be found." Hindu lawbooks indicate that gambling is among the most serious of vices and renders a person impure. Furthermore, it is taught that "the wealth obtained by gambling is tainted." (*Encyclopedia of Religion* 1928)

Buddhist

Siddhartha Gautama was born into a rich Nepalese family in 568 B.C. and led a young life of relative leisure. However, when he was 29 years old he experienced a series of visions that led to events which eventually brought the Buddhist religion to more than a billion people in South Asia and China. Gautama's three images—an old man, a sick man, and a dead man—convinced him that the world was full of suffering. He also saw a vision of a wandering holy man and became convinced that he, too, would have to wander in order to find the path leading out of suffering.

Gautama cast off his life of leisure and left his family in search of truth. At first he was convinced he would have to live an existence of poverty and self-denial. His initial lack of success led to despair and meditation, but in time Gautama came to know the enlightenment for which he quested. With this enlightenment he became the Buddha—the one filled with truth—and began to preach to others about the Middle Path. This path lay between total self-denial, with its rejection of the world, and a non-contemplative worldly life. For five decades the Buddha travelled through Nepal and India attracting followers, establishing temples, and instructing people about the Middle Path.

Buddha taught that the world was burdened with suffering as a result of desire. If we desire and are not satisfied, he said, we know the suffering of frustration, but if we do achieve our wants and are satisfied, we shall only begin to desire more and will become preoccupied with fears that others will take our achievements away. We suffer in cycles that persist from birth to death and then again through new births and new deaths. These cycles can only be broken with enlightenment. A person who has reached enlightenment or the level of a Buddha, can ascend to a state of Nirvana, which is a condition of utter happiness and peace. With death, then, such a person arrives in a heaven-like resting place.

Buddha and others who reached enlightenment gave many instructions about the Middle Path. The Buddha first had to achieve an existence of perfect virtue. The ten "perfections" of the Buddhas included generosity, self-sacrifice, morality, renunciation, wisdom, energy, forbearance, truthfulness, resoluteness, loving kindness, and equanimity. (Spiro 1982) These perfections were obtained through a rejection of worldly passions and an embracement of good deeds.

The instructions for the Middle Path required attention to the Noble Eightfold Path: knowledge of the truth, intentions to resist evil, saying nothing to harm others, respecting life and morality, holding a job that doesn't hurt others, freeing the mind of evil, controlling feelings and thought, and practicing proper forms of concentration. (*World Book Encyclopedia* 1978)

The path to enlightenment could be blocked by frivolous and sinful actions. Participation in gambling activity only served to lead one away from the Middle Path. Since gambling heightens passions and desires, it is to be avoided. In one account of Buddha's instructions, the *Parabhava Sutta,* the addictions to dice, strong drink, and women are listed among the "means whereby men are brought to loss." In the *Tevijja Sutta,* monks, who closely followed Buddha, were warned that spectacles, games, contests using animals, and dice are addictive distractions which destroy virtue. (*Encyclopedia of Religion* 1928)

Buddhist laymen are instructed to avoid six things that are said to contribute to loss of virtue: liquor, feasts, bad companions, laziness, "walking in the streets at untimely hours," and gambling. (Morgan 1956)

Buddhism, like Hinduism, observes many gods, but Buddhist gods have a functional purpose of steering devout followers in the right direction. These gods are people who have achieved enlightenment during their time on earth, and unlike the gods of Hindu mythology, they continue to lead their lives as models for others to emulate. Part of this model behavior includes abstinence from gambling.

Shinto

The Shinto religion of Japan emerged after hundreds of years of contact with Buddhism. In many senses Shinto beliefs and practices are amalgamations of Buddhism and other Eastern systems of religious thought, including Confucianism. Many of the gods worshiped in Shinto temples are also Buddhist gods. Shintoism was different in that it nearly became a state-sanctioned religion when it took on very nationalistic characteristics in the 1800s. This occurred partly because the Emperor of Japan was considered a descendent of the Sun God. Also, unlike Buddhism, Shinto gods were considered entities that could help the Japanese achieve worldly goods and desires. Nevertheless, many Buddhist precepts remain embedded in Shintoism, and gambling is condemned by the religion as an activity that diverts one from the path to virtue and righteousness.

Pros and Cons of Legalized Gambling

Legal campaigns to win approval for various forms of gambling are usually argued around three basic issues: economics, crime, and compulsive behavior. Moral issues such as those outlined in the preceding section do not generally dominate contemporary discussions of gambling, although they were very important at one time as a roadblock to legalization.

The most compelling issue advanced by proponents of legalized gambling involves economics. Gambling advocates invariably present the argument that gaming activity will generate new funds for public treasuries that can be spent on myriad worthy causes, and also create jobs and general economic growth in the community. They stress that gambling taxes are politically more acceptable than other forms of taxation because they are paid voluntarily by the gamblers themselves.

Gambling proponents seek to minimize concerns about crime by emphasizing that gambling is best controlled when it is legal. Legalization, they say, drives criminals from such enterprises.

Often, gaming advocates exploit law enforcement resources as a political issue. They suggest that people will gamble whether it is legal or not, thereby taxing precious police enforcement resources needed for the more urgent problems of murder, rape, robbery, and arson. This argument basically holds, too, that laws prohibiting gambling are basically unenforceable.

Gambling supporters also insist that problems related to compulsive gambling affect only a very small portion of the population, and that these people can be kept away from gambling institutions and treated for their behavior.

Opponents of legalized gambling are always ready to dispute these points. They counter that gambling taxes are not truly voluntary, and that job creation and predictions of economic growth are only illusory.

Moreover, opponents see legal gambling as a catalyst for many kinds of criminal activity, rather than a tool that will help free police resources to fight serious crime. This side of the debate views gambling as a personally destructive activity which leads many to pathological behavior when they lose control over their wagering addiction. Gambling opponents prophesy a decay of social responsibility in communities that sanction gambling.

Economics

There can be little debate over gambling's economic impact on society. A lot of money changes hands each day in America through gambling, and more than $300 billion is wagered each year in legal games. Gamblers lose well over $30 billion each year or, put another way, gambling enterprises win over $30 billion annually. This volume of money dwarfs the $8 billion spent in the recorded music industry each year and the $5 billion paid by moviegoers and video renters each year. Clearly, gambling is the number one entertainment industry in terms of cash flow and profit.

Many gambling proceeds do find their way into public treasuries. With tax benefits at the top of the proponents' justification lists for legalization, a closer examination of gambling taxes is warranted.

An effective tax should, first and foremost, generate money for the public welfare. Do gambling taxes churn up sizable revenues for deposit in government accounts? The aggregate revenue from gaming nationally probably falls somewhere between $9 billion and $10 billion. Certainly this is a lot of dollar power for public programs. Does this money go a long way toward satisfying the fiscal needs of the states? In sum, state revenues amounted to just over $300 billion in 1990, which meant that gaming revenues accounted for just over 3 percent of the total. As a revenue generator, gambling ranked sixth behind general sales taxes ($99 billion), individual income taxes ($96 billion), corporate taxes ($22 billion), gasoline taxes ($19 billion), and license fees ($19 billion). Gambling revenues did, however, exceed those of death taxes, severance taxes, property taxes, and tobacco and alcohol taxes. (Council of State Governments 1992)

The importance of gambling as a revenue source can also be assessed by examining situations in individual states. In Nevada, the $370 million brought in through direct casino win taxes amounted to 42 percent of the state's tax revenues. (Other taxes relating to gaming and tourism—for instance, sales taxes paid by visitors—bring the estimated figure to over 50 percent). However, in New Jersey, casino taxes provide only 2.2 percent of the funds for state coffers. When New Jersey adds its lottery revenue and horse race tax revenues to this, the percentage of state revenue from gambling climbs to almost 6 percent.

A survey of 1988 revenues showed that none of the 48 remaining states secured a higher portion of revenues from gaming. Lotteries, for instance, yielded a maximum of 4.7 percent of the total for Maryland, while the average was closer to 2.1 percent. In many states, lottery taxes yielded less than 1 percent of the revenues. Horse racing revenues also represented small portions of state treasuries. In New Hampshire, taxes on horse racing produced just over 3 percent of the state total; only in four additional states did horse racing buttress the state's wallet by as much as 1 percent. (Mikesell and Zorn 1986)

While such revenue totals are not significant in terms of the overall spending equation, proceeds from gaming taxes in some areas are earmarked for specific purposes, such as parks, education, or tax relief for seniors. In these cases, of course, the proportion of revenues contributed by gambling levies is much greater. However, state policy makers have time and time again refused to increase spending on specific projects or programs when gambling revenues are earmarked for such activities. Instead, the tendency is to reduce general fund contributions to the project by the sum of gambling revenue produced. In effect, then, nearly all gambling taxes must be considered as mere components of a states' amalgamated funds and not principal funding resources for projects or services.

As such, gambling taxes make a real difference only in Nevada. Gaming revenues there are potential funding powerhouses for individual charities and for small organizations or governments. Bingo games have been effective in raising funds for a variety of charities, private schools, and hospitals, and Nevada. Indian reservations have gained quite large sums of money through gambling. Indeed, almost all Nevada tribes that permit gambling have discovered these operations to be the strongest reservation employers and the leading source of funding. This is a function of the small population of most reservations.

A second criterion for assessing the worthiness of a tax is its reliability. Governments can plan ahead for anticipated sums of revenue from reliable levies that have shown themselves to provide stable yields year after year. Generally, Nevada casino tax revenues have demonstrated solid reliability and have consistently grown between the 1950s and the 1990s. Still, it is not unheard of for budget authorities to miscalculate estimated tax yields, giving rise to occasional fiscal crises.

For many years, lotteries appeared to be excellent revenue sources for the states that permitted them. From the inception of lottery programs and into the 1980s, double-digit revenue growth occurred in many locations. However, these revenue gains did not last, and some states have experienced revenue declines.

Clotfelter and Cook's in-depth study of lotteries found that collectively lotteries have the greatest volatility when compared to other tax systems, but not that much greater than sales taxes, income taxes, or other state revenue sources. (Clotfelter and Cook 1989)

A passive lottery game was instituted in Illinois in 1974, and an instant game followed the next year. Sales of lottery products increased from $129 million to $163 million in the second year. Encouraged, the Illinois legislature wrote budgets that anticipated additional revenue growth, but at the same time the novelty of playing the lottery began to wear off, and for the next three years sales fell 60 percent.

A similar situation seems to be occurring in California, where 1992 lottery sales declined 17 percent from the previous year. The California scramble is now on to adjust marketing strategies in an attempt to rebuild sales.

Another measure of an effective tax relates to the efficiency of revenue collection. Gambling taxes pose a problem here, because some operators have been successful in hiding revenues. This, however, is not a major difficulty. Most gaming enterprises do pay the required amount of taxes owed—especially government-run lotteries.

The administrative cost of collecting casino taxes varies considerably between the two biggest casino states. Of course, not all casino regulation is oriented toward tax collection, but regulation is necessary to keep the industry operating properly. New Jersey spends approximately $80 million annually for casino regulation. This amount is charged back to the casinos and should be subtracted from the aggregate casino revenues of $228 million. In other words, regulatory and collection costs amount to 35 percent of the statewide revenue generated. New Jersey pays 35 cents for each revenue dollar it brings in from a casino.

Nevada's system exhibits greater efficiency. The states spends about $20 million in administration to collect $370 million in revenues—only 5.4 percent of the total, or six cents on the dollar.

Pari-mutuel systems usually operate on a share basis. Out of the pool of money wagered by the betting public, 85 percent may be returned to the bettors. The remainder is split between track operators, horse-racing associations, horse owners (including prizes for race winners), and the state government. These three groups may each get 5 percent in a typical split. Operators pay the costs of regulation and collection. The efficiency of this system is comparable to that of the New Jersey casinos.

In general, the efficiency of lottery sources as revenue generators leaves something to be desired. Collection and administration costs range from a low of 18 cents on the dollar in Maryland to *more* than a dollar in Colorado, Montana, and Kansas. Canadian governments typically spend 43 cents. In fiscal 1989, United States lotteries spent about $2.1 billion to raise and collect $7.3 billion for various government treasuries—a 23.1 percent chunk of the revenues.

The taxation issue raised most vociferously in lottery debates is that of equity. If the purpose of lotteries is to raise money for government, it is prudent to ask whether that revenue is being drawn from the people who can most afford to pay for government services. The answer: probably not.

Many lottery studies suggest that the game appeals to certain segments of the population more than others. One study found that 65 percent of lottery tickets were purchased by 10 percent of the population. For example, ticket purchasers in California were more likely than not to be less educated or hold low-paying jobs. (Mangalmurti and Cooke 1991)

Since the poor account for a greater share of lottery ticket purchases, taxes on those purchases are considered regressive. Economist Daniel Suits found that in Massachusetts people with annual incomes below $5,000 drew 1.9 percent of the state's individual income while purchasing 8.9 percent of the lottery tickets. Connecticut citizens earning under $10,000 a year commanded an 8 percent share of state income and a 20 percent share of lottery sales. In a tax index developed by Suits, lotteries in such states appeared to be the most regressive form of taxation. (Mangalmurti and Cooke 1991)

Other scholars have found similar results. John Mikesell and Kurt Zorn concluded that "lotteries place a greater relative burden on low-income families, because low-income groups spend a higher percentage of their income on lottery tickets than do high-income groups. The spending pattern has been found frequently." (Mikesell and Zorn 1986)

One reason explaining the higher incidence of play among poor citizens is the method in which lotteries are marketed. Much advertising portrays the game as a plausible, easy, even recommended way of escaping the rut of poverty. Such merchandising ploys send the message that success can be achieved painlessly, without hard work or perseverance. (Mangalmurti and Cooke 1991)

State lottery bureaucrats know the poor are vulnerable to these kinds of appeals and install more lottery sales outlets in poor neighborhoods. One Delaware study found that lottery sales stations were almost nonexistent in the high-income areas outside of Wilmington, with one ticket dispensing machine for every 17,714 persons, while in working-class neighborhoods machines were available for every 5,032 residents and in lower-income areas there was a machine for every 1,981 people. (Mangalmurti and Cooke 1991)

Similarly, a 1984 study in Maryland discovered one lottery outlet for every 1,850 Baltimore residents, a city with average household incomes of $16,800. Yet Montgomery County, where families averaged $34,000 annually, contained a lottery station for every 5,800 residents. (Karcher 1989) Another study found similar distribution inequities in and around Detroit.

Legalized gambling is often suggested as a remedy for unemployment. The claim that gambling is a producer of jobs is confined largely to casino operations. George Sternlieb and James Hughes observed that "the promise of increased employment played the largest part in winning endorsement for casino gambling [in New Jersey]." (Sternlieb and Hughes 1983) Likewise, the battle cry of casino advocates in Chicago is "Jobs! Jobs! Jobs!" A proposed $2 billion casino complex there has been touted as the route to 57,000 new jobs. Another 25,000 new positions were projected for a New Orleans casino project.

Are these numbers realistic? It isn't an easy question, but we can look at some road signs in our attempt to find an answer. Certainly more jobs will be created by casino projects that attract tourists because the gamblers will need additional services. Jobs may also be generated through construction activity, but this economic shot in the arm may later be revealed as transitory. If construction materials, labor, and casino workers are imported, the promise of additional jobs and lasting economic gain will have turned out to be a pipe dream. Moreover, construction company profits may or may not remain in the community following completion of the project, and construction materials may not even be supplied locally. In such scenarios, communities run the risk of boom-bust cycles that can temporarily disrupt the social calm and, later, leave a bitter aftertaste.

Job-related questions other than those related to quantity must be considered when deciding which stand to take on gambling propositions. What kinds of jobs? Will they be skilled, lucrative positions, or minimum-wage entry level positions? Are the local unemployed eligible? How stable will these positions be?

An assessment of these concerns in Atlantic City points to mixed results. New casinos there did provide more than 40,000 jobs, but most of them were awarded to applicants who lived outside the economically depressed city. In fact, the unemployment picture in Atlantic City proper did not change materially after the casinos arrived. Evidence also showed that the hotels in most cases did not produce highly motivated work atmospheres because the jobs paid on the low end of the scale.

There were some upsides to the situation. Young, unskilled applicants were able to move into many of the new positions quickly, and some skilled jobs were created. These higher responsibility slots were the kinds that demanded applicants with high integrity.

There is a grim possibility connected to the proliferation of gaming sites across the country. Suppose casinos are overbuilt in certain locations and the availability of facilities exceeds the demand for gambling? These new casinos could fall flat. Even in Las Vegas and Atlantic City, big casinos have failed even while the general gambling scene has remained stable, or even grown. Other than bankruptcy lawyers, there are few winners when a casino goes under.

Crime

When asked why he robbed banks, the notorious Willie Sutton replied simply: "That's where the money is!" So it is with thieves. They can smell money. To some of them, gambling establishments are almost like banks. Players bring their money to the casinos, bingo halls, race tracks, and lottery agents, and this money trades hands continuously. This necessitates a constant tracking of cash flow. But the wagers placed at busy gambling halls can move at such a dizzying, intoxicating pace, and in such great volume, that perceptions regarding the true value of currency can almost metamorphose into a deception. In this process, fiscal controls may loosen, both on the part of the operators' monitoring systems and the players' capacity for restraint. We must remind ourselves that crime is a basic function of opportunity. (Cloward and Ohlin 1960) It gravitates toward money, and the more that money is fast-moving and loosely controlled, the more crime seems to gravitate toward gambling.

It is therefore no surprise that crime is often the loudest cry shouted by detractors over the din of the gambling debate. Opponents of legalized casinos view organized crime as the real businessmen in charge, while street criminals roam the environs of gaming establishments. Opponents portray race tracks as havens where contest results are determined as often by manipulation and cheating as by fair competition. Even lotteries and charity operations are not exempt from accusations of dishonesty.

Gambling apologists generally try to dodge the crime issue by emphasizing that their plans call for the strictest government controls. They point out that legal gambling with controls is preferable to illegal gambling without them. Indeed, gambling supporters will even attempt to sell the legalization alternative as an effective political mechanism for shooing criminal elements from the business.

Heavy exploitation of the crime issue comes into play when casino propositions are debated. Opponents usually argue that organized crime will eventually assume control of the legal casinos. Virgil Peterson, a longtime head of the Chicago Crime Commission, claimed that the "underworld inevitably gains a foothold under any licensing system. If state authorities establish the vast policing system rigid supervision requires, the underworld merely provides itself with fronts who obtain the licenses, with actual ownership remaining in its own hands; and it receives a major share of the profits." (Peterson 1951)

New Jersey authorities certainly hoped things wouldn't turn out that way when gambling was approved in 1976. When Governor Brendan Byrne signed the new licensing and regulation law, he declared in no uncertain terms that "organized crime is not welcome. I warn them: keep your filthy hands out of Atlantic City." But, alas, Byrne's words flew to the wind. (Pollock 1987; DeMaris 1986)

From its initial involvement in casino licensing, New Jersey compromised its ability to control organized crime. The state attorney general's office investigated the first applicant, Resorts International, and concluded that the company was financed by underworld bosses and had a record of bribery and skimming in its Bahamas casino. The attorney general asked that the license be denied, but New Jersey's Casino Control Commission overruled the recommendation, reasoning that such an action would represent a severe economic setback for Atlantic City, whose leaders were eager to start reaping the benefits of the new industry. (Sternlieb and Hughes 1983)

It wasn't only wise-guy casino operators who created problems: Organized crime was found to be pervasive all over Atlantic City in junket operations, credit scams, slot machine cheating, laundering schemes for narcotics money, labor unions, and ancillary industries. The stench of crime even led investigators to the offices of the mayor and a United States senator.

The Federal Bureau of Investigation, suspecting that things were going awry, cast their net of attention over Atlantic City. In 1979 the FBI began a sting operation called ABSCAM, which was short for "Abdul Scam." (DeMaris 1986; Pollock 1987) Agents posed as Arab sheiks representing the fictitious Abdul Enterprises. They offered bribes to United States Senator Harrison Williams, six Congressmen, and to New Jersey politicians, including gaming regulators, along with a request for favorable consideration for a casino license. As the money traded hands, assurances were given that the license would be forthcoming. A literal who's who of notables in the state's licensing offices were named on secret tape recordings. Senator Williams was convicted of bribery, and Casino Control Commission Chairman Joseph Lordi and Vice Chairman Kenneth MacDonald resigned. Following a separate investigation, Atlantic City Mayor Michael J. Matthews was convicted and sentenced to a 15-year sentence for accepting bribes and payoffs from the Nicodemo (Little Nicky) Scarfo crime organization. (DeMaris 1986)

In the process, federal attorneys painted a dismal portrait of the early years of New Jersey casino gaming. Attorney Robert Del Tufo suggested that "we have two governors in New Jersey. The one administration is that elected by the people. The other administration is that designated by the leaders of organized crime. . . . [It] is a government that lives off blood money and drug money and rules from the alleys and back rooms and the shadowy places you and I never go. No party—and no candidate—can lay legitimate claim to the first government of New Jersey until it deals with the second." (DeMaris 1986)

The New Jersey state police superintendent found that illegal sports betting increased substantially after casinos opened in Atlantic City. Crime families from Massachusetts, Pennsylvania, and New York conducted their operations in and around the casinos. One special FBI agent claimed that up to ten Mafia "families" were involved in "unions, junkets, and other ancillary businesses" connected with the city's casino scene. (DeMaris 1986)

At another level, below that of organized crime, lurks a different kind of casino crook. These characters stalk the ongoing games, assessing their opportunities to cheat the casinos or other players. Cheats work alone, in teams, and sometimes in confederacy with casino employees.

On roulette and craps tables they use sleight of hand to post bets after plays have been completed. They also change the amounts of their bets by "top hatting" stacks of chips which have already been placed. At blackjack, these individuals use mirrors and other devices to watch a dealer's play and calculate the odds.

The slot machines of today offer more opportunity for cheaters than ever before. With progressive jackpots exceeding $8 million, the schemers are staying up late to plan their next move. Even though slot machine manufacturers claim to have introduced "foolproof" designs, cheaters have managed to prevail. Even casino dealers have entered the cheating game by playing cat and mouse with the Internal Revenue Service as they seek to hide tips from the tax collector.

Not all casino crime relates directly to gaming. Casinos attract people who tend to carry large sums of cash on their persons, and there are those few who are lucky enough to parley small sums into large wads of currency that they must carry out of the casino. These people become attractive targets for thieves and prostitutes. The high crime rates in Atlantic City and Las Vegas suggest that the criminals know where to find such victims.

Gaming proponents don't accept the negative side of the crime argument without rebuttal, however. They continue to point out that the incidence of mob activity has been drastically reduced in recent years. As corporations have assumed control of casino facilities with capital values approaching a billion dollars, every effort has been made to ensure that operations are clean and clear of mob influence. Nevada authorities have pulled the licenses of operations such as the Aladdin, the Stardust, the Fremont, and the Sundance casinos—all medium-sized Las Vegas properties. This suggests that government will tolerate little from those who wish to be dishonest players in this lucrative industry. When a company has invested hundreds of millions of dollars in a casino facility, a license is critical. When it comes to obtaining and keeping a license, honesty is the best policy.

Corporations are also acutely aware that they will lose patronage if the public suspects gambling in their casinos is manipulated in any way. For this reason, casinos install state-of-the-art surveillance equipment to make sure they will not suffer at the hands of cheaters, be they players or employees.

In addition, gambling proponents have challenged the gambling-associated street crime statistics that are bandied about in anti-gambling arguments. Close analyses of crime patterns in Atlantic City and Las Vegas have served to discount some erroneous conclusions about the casino-crime connection. True, crime rates rose in Atlantic City after the introduction of casinos, but casinos weren't the only contributing factor.

A study by Ronald Ochrym compared gaming communities with other tourist destinations that did not have casinos. Ochrym found that rates of crime were similar. Crime, in fact, seems to be more a function of the influx of tourists than it is an adjunct of casino gambling. While crime statistics did soar following the introduction of casinos in Atlantic City, so too did crime in Orlando, Florida, following the opening of Disneyworld. If the casinos themselves are thought to cause crime, gaming backers scoff, so does Mickey Mouse. (Ochrym and Park 1990)

More than 30 million visitors come to Atlantic City each year. Many do not know which areas of town to avoid and may unwittingly set themselves up as vulnerable targets. Such crime is difficult to prosecute due to the inconvenience and expense of bringing tourists back to the city to serve as witnesses for investigations and trials.

Gaming proponents note that surveillance activity in gambling establishments is very expensive, as is the prosecution of slippery operators. They acknowledge the reluctance of judges and juries to convict and punish nonviolent gambling culprits. With gambling legalization, goes the argument, shady game operators will quit the business of their own volition, liberating police resources to battle society's harsher criminal elements.

Adherents to this rationale like to parallel it with the historic effect that the halt of alcohol prohibition had on liquor-related crime. When bans on the sale and consumption of alcohol ended with the repeal of the Eighteenth Amendment (executed by adoption of the Twenty-First Amendment), illegal merchandising of alcohol ceased for the most part, and thereafter most drinkers sought their pleasures in legal establishments.

Another analogous situation that can be useful to the position of gambling supporters was Nevada's legalization of gaming in 1931. Prior to that date, illegal activities were rampant in the back rooms of taverns. Legalization brought games operators back to the front of the bar, where they advertised gambling openly. The state proceeded to license and modestly tax these operators, who were quite happy that they no longer had to bribe local officials to stay open.

In a similar vein, the Betting and Gaming Act of 1960 worked to eliminate illegal bookie operations in England. British government by and large eradicated illegal betting merely by requiring the bookies that ran horse- and sports-betting enterprises to set up and license permanent locations inside commercial buildings. The British required licensing fees, but no gaming taxes. (Dixon 1988)

Unfortunately, things don't always work so smoothly. In order to use legalization as a tool in the elimination of illegal gambling, certain conditions must be met. The overriding consideration is that the newly legal method of gambling must duplicate, or at least be very much like, the illegal activity it replaces— including rules of operation, marketing, products, locations, and times of business—or else the new game will require a lot of policing.

A case in point is the typical state lottery. State lotteries have not successfully driven illegal numbers games out of business, although this has been one of the explicitly stated purposes for offering them under the government umbrella. In illegal numbers rackets, players select a three or four digit number which must match a drawn number in order to win. The government-blessed version of this game, however, is not set up the same way, which helps explain why it has failed to drive the illegal numbers games out of existence. For one thing, payoffs from the illegal games are often better than those from government lotteries, and clandestine numbers operators also have a reputation for better customer service. They do, after all, think of themselves as businessmen and not bureaucrats. These operators will take bets over the telephone, allow play on credit, and deliver cash prizes to a winner's doorstep when the tax man is not looking.

Robert Wagman explains that efforts to get rid of the illegal operators may actually be achieving the opposite effect:

> Actually, some law enforcement officials are now saying that indications are that the lottery may actually be helping the illegal game. Players are being introduced to the numbers concept in the state-run game, then they switch to the illegal game when they realize they can get a better deal. Then too, the legal state game has solved the perennial problem faced by the illegal games of finding a commonly accepted, and widely available, three-digit number to pay off on. Most of the illegal street games now simply use the state's pick-3 number. (Wagman 1986)

Illegal numbers have gained at least three advantages with the onset of government lotteries. First, customers of illegal games can now rest assured that selection of the winning number is random and honest. Secondly, customers can now quickly learn the winning number, which is aired almost immediately on radio and television and printed in the daily newspaper. This helps operators deliver prizes to winners more efficiently. Third, undercover operators can now "lay-off" bets when customers play heavily on particular numbers. That is, they can offset their risks of losing by simply going to the legal lotteries and betting the same numbers as their customers.

The author's study of Dutch casinos found that legalization was accompanied by an increase in illegal casino activity. Because the Netherlands also decided that the government should run the legal casinos, illegal operators were not provided open access to the market place. They were not given the opportunity to convert from an illegal to a legal mode of operation. Neither could they be co-opted by the government and given positions in the new casinos, because policy makers decided that those who had worked in illegal houses should be disqualified from government casino employment. (Thompson and Pinney 1990)

While the Dutch government felt it could defeat illicit operators by competing with them, they nevertheless yielded to a negative public viewpoint of the new casinos. While the public had signed off on the idea of casinos as deterrents to surreptitious games, it still did not like the idea of gambling houses per se. Legal casinos were forced to abstain from advertising and were located in remote areas. They were pressured to enforce dress codes, charge entrance fees, and limit their hours. This had the ironic effect of making the government houses very uncompetitive, which had not been the objective in the first place. Instead of scrambling for market share that the government had intended to snatch from them through legalization, the clandestine operators thrived. They actually gained market share by standing outside the legal casinos at closing time with handbills directing customers to 24-hour gaming houses. Moreover, attorneys were able to persuade judges that those illegal operators who did get rounded up for court were not criminals—only competitive businessmen.

A parallel scenario occurred in Australia when the government sought to eliminate illegal bookies by establishing government-operated sports-betting shops. These shops only stimulated the demand for illegal sport betting activity. (Dixon 1990)

This is not to say that legalization is unworkable as a damper on illegal gambling, but such ploys must be executed skillfully. By their very nature, legitimate gambling operations must be capable of satisfying the particulars of public demand or they will serve only to stimulate more of the activity they are designed to eradicate.

Problem Gamblers

While many are willing to debate the suggestion that gambling offers positive social redemptions, few would disagree that, as a habit, it can be a very destructive force in individual lives. People get hooked on gambling, almost like they do on drugs or alcohol. They lose fortunes. Some may borrow and steal to support their habit, and sadly, some have lost all hope and committed suicide.

The issue of compulsive gambling arises whenever the activity becomes a political issue. Horrible examples of obsessive gambling and self-destruction are exposed in anti-gaming advertisements. However, while these may help illustrate a problem area, they do not illuminate. More fundamental considerations are at work in the problem gambler than the symptoms of his compulsion. Why do people become addicted to this risky activity? How do they devolve to this level? Which games draw them in, and where do they play? How many potential problem gamblers are there and what can be done to treat them?

In 1974, the Commission on the Review of the National Policy Toward Gambling conducted a survey that indicated 61 percent of the American adult population had participated in gambling that year. This suggested that the United States contained some 100 million gamblers. Naturally, most of these people did not have a serious problem with gambling, or any problem at all, because most individuals who take gambling risks are aware of the financial perils that await them. Most gamblers, in fact, behave in a rational manner when they play. They have decided they are willing to risk losses in exchange for the thrill of the diversion. Some have even learned the odds well enough to gain a level of wagering skill that earns them money.

Others, however, have been known to take leave of their reason upon entering the fantasy world of popping lights, ringing bells, and clinking coins. Some of these personality types, caught in an atmosphere of inflated hope, may seek out individuals with similar character traits and gambling habits. The most obsessive and compulsive of the gamblers may become so entranced as to lose awareness of the very people and activity that surrounds them. At this point the lines that demarcate pure wishfulness and true probability vanish, and they begin to live the game instead of the reality.

Traditionally, people with dominant gambling habits were viewed as morally deprived. This overly simple view of problem gambling was first challenged by Sigmund Freud and his colleagues. Freud analyzed the writings of Fyodor Dostoyevsky, author of *The Gambler,* which was thought to be autobiographical, and reasoned that Dostoyevsky's frantic behavior had risen from a desire for self-punishment. Later studies along these same lines concluded that certain kinds of gamblers derived a masochistic pleasure from losing. (Freud 1928)

In 1980, the American Psychiatric Association endorsed a medical model of pathological gambling symptoms and defined the problem as a disorder of impulse control. This "disease," it said, exhibited many of the same attributes as other addictions, notably alcohol and drug dependency.

Several conditions were necessary to flesh out an individual's diagnosis as a pathological gambler. These could include:

1. Frequent preoccupation with gambling or with securing money in order to gamble
2. Gambling more aggressively or longer than planned

3. A need to increase the size and/or frequency
   of bets to obtain the desired level of excitement
4. Restlessness and irritability during periods of
   gambling inactivity
5. The desire to chase losses with more frequent
   and higher bets
6. Frequent efforts to stop gambling
7. Gambles even when other obligations are
   pressing
8. Gambles without regard to increasing debt

Most treatment programs set up for problem gamblers have accepted this medical definition, suggesting that pathological gambling is often a permanent, irreversible condition. The best cure, it has been determined, is abstinence—total, complete, and permanent. A return to the activity at any level is likely to bring on the full problem once more. Just as the alcoholic must cure himself by never again imbibing in a single drink, the addicted gambler who seeks a remedy must never place another bet.

Gamblers Anonymous is a program that utilizes group therapy and personal support to assist problem gamblers and encourage them to stay away from the action. In 1972 a local chapter of the organization in Ohio requested that a nearby Veterans Administration Medical Center start an inpatient program for compulsive gamblers. This was the first such program in the United States. (Rosecrance 1988) Other groups bound together that same year to form the National Council on Compulsive Gambling, an organization that advocates support programs based upon the above-mentioned medical conditions. The group has successfully lobbied state governments to win funding for its programs. Maryland, New York, New Jersey, Connecticut, and Iowa, among other states, finance these programs from gambling tax revenues.

The American Psychiatric Association model and Gamblers Anonymous treatment methods, however, are not universally accepted. Sociologist John Rosecrance has suggested that psychiatrists and clinicians defined the criterion for pinpointing compulsive players by studying and treating mostly those problem gamblers who were profoundly affected. Rosecrance asserted that these were individuals that had completely surrendered their will and would have been viewed as unusual even by other gamblers with financially debilitating, albeit less serious, habits.

Rosecrance could claim intimate familiarity with the phenomenon he studied. He spent his adult years as a race enthusiast, betting heavily, and often more than he could afford. He won and he lost, and generally made the betting parlor his alternative social existence. As a scholar and observer of this scene, Rosecrance was acquainted with many other habitual gamblers—people that might have been called compulsive by others. Rosecrance realized they were not truly compulsive—they pursued their recreation with both feet firmly grounded, even when the betting became irrational or they lost, and they would engage each other with psychological coping mechanisms. While they were detached from the outside world, these players, unlike the severely strung out gambling loner, never completely lost sight of their desperate circumstances while keeping their own company. (Rosecrance 1988)

Rosecrance felt that losing huge amounts of money is the chief reason that some addicted gamblers become despondent. People tend to become emotionally and mentally unbalanced as they lose money, but the distress of a losing gambler never manifests in exactly the same way. Some are quite capable of quitting early; some may quit a bit later, and some who stay the course are lucky enough to begin winning again. These players may also be capable of stopping before losing their good fortune again.

Rosecrance concluded that there are many types of problem gamblers and said their treatment should take into account the social setting and their reasons for seeking such an alternative setting. The solution to the problem of obsession, he suggested, need not be total abstinence. Rosecrance advocated more gradual withdrawals, counseling to help habitual gamblers learn to play with less money, and counseling to assist in the understanding of personal problems involving spouses, children, or jobs. These kinds of difficulties, he reasoned, lay at the heart of the gambler's flight from the responsibilities of life. The better a gambler is at learning to take control of his life, the more likely it is that person will evolve from a desperate to a responsible gambler.

How many pathological gamblers are there, and how many are prone to enter this condition? It is important to know the extent of problem gambling in any society. But we should realize that there are a host of other habit-forming activities that damage peoples' health and lives and are not subject to control. Millions of people enjoy alcohol, coffee, tobacco, sugar, and fatty foods. These things are ingested legally and voluntarily. Some people cannot control their intake, and may suffer harm—even death—

from car accidents, obesity, or lung cancer. Just because a few individuals cannot control their indulgences, should society ban these items carte blanche? Other people enjoy the same products in moderation. So, too, do millions of people enjoy gambling without falling to ruin. The weakness of a few does not justify the punishment of many.

Policy makers must decide the severity of a problem before banning a product or earmarking public funding for treatment programs. Also, sensitivity to the scope of the problem can help them institute proper controls within the gaming industries. Of course, if a potential problem looks especially ominous, it is best to err on the side of caution and deny legalization of gambling.

As a mass-marketed phenomenon, gambling today would pose a potentially serious problem for society if a large number of people were evaluated as probable addicts. If it is thought that few are inclined in this direction, the potential for difficulty is naturally much smaller. At any rate, some people are bound to be affected. Knowing the probable extent of the problem would allow rule makers to determine the amount of financial burden that should be levied on gambling operators to finance treatment of the afflicted. If a large number of players were seen to be cultivating unhealthy gambling patterns, perhaps additional restrictions on players, gambling operations, and gambling advertising would be justified. For instance, people could be required to identify themselves when purchasing lottery tickets, or tickets could be tracked in the same way that certain prescription drugs are tracked. With such methods we could help assure that gamblers do not exceed their means or do not gamble with others' resources.

If a problem-prone population is large enough, we can establish self-choice or family-choice mechanisms for exclusion from the ability to purchase gambling products. Or, we can restrict credit gambling by requiring that people gamble only with funds they physically bring into a gaming establishment. We can restrict the distribution of alcoholic beverages, and most importantly, we can make efforts to keep our children away from gambling activity.

If, on the other hand, the problem-prone population is determined to be fairly small, we should closely and carefully consider whether to deprive the population at large from partaking in recreational gambling. Personal freedom and choice are cherished values in our society, and Americans should care about preserving them.

How big is the potential for large-scale problem gambling? This is an important question for policy makers. Estimations of the numbers of compulsive or potentially compulsive gamblers vary widely—from less than 1 percent to more than 7 percent. The earliest estimates from Gamblers Anonymous suggested that there were between six and nine million pathological gamblers in the United States. Dr. Robert Custer calculated that 2 percent of adult males were compulsive gamblers, while one-tenth of that proportion of females were compulsives.

The first comprehensive national survey on compulsive gambling was conducted for the National Policy Commission by the Survey Research Center of the University of Michigan in 1975. Researchers concluded that .77 percent of the adult population consisted of probable problem gamblers, while another 2.33 percent were potentially compulsive gamblers. They suggested that just over one million people were compulsives, whereas nearly four million would be if gambling was widely accessible to the full population. (Commission on the Review of the National Policy Toward Gambling 1976)

An Ohio study in 1984 put the incidence of pathological gambling among adults at 2.5 percent, while a Rutgers University survey of Philadelphia area (in New Jersey) residents indicated that as many as 7.5 percent had problems with gambling and that 3.4 percent, or just under half that total, could be considered compulsive gamblers. They suggested that the proportion of problem gamblers increased rapidly after casino gaming came to Atlantic City. (Taber, Collachi, and Lynn 1986)

The debate over the numbers will continue, but even with the lower estimates, proponents of gambling should not let the matter rest. Their argument that the lot should not be punished for the indiscretions of a few has merit, and it is not only gamblers who are hurt by irresponsible players. Leisure and Custer write: "We would estimate that between 10 and 15 persons are directly affected by the typical pathological gambler, including spouse, children, parents, and other close relatives, fellow gamblers, people borrowed from and stolen from, employers and employees." (Lesieur and Custer 1984) Gambling proponents should be able to assert that the form of gambling that is proposed will contain safeguards to minimize the effects of compulsive behaviors on communities, and also that treatment programs—whether based on the medical model or some other behavioral modification model, as recommended by Rosecrance's research—are available for those that will suffer from the presence of gambling in the community.

References

Abt, Vicki, James F. Smith, and Eugene Martin Christiansen, *The Business of Risk: Commercial Gambling in Mainstream America* (Lawrence: University Press of Kansas, 1985).

Bashman, A.L., *The Wonder That Was India* (Calcutta: Rupa Company, 1967).

Bell, Raymond, "Moral Views on Gambling Promulgated by Major American Religious Bodies." In *Gambling in America: Appendix 1*, edited by the Commission on the Review of National Policy on Gambling. (Washington, DC: Superintendent of Documents, Government Printing Office, 1976).

Berger, A.J., and Nancy Bruning, *Lady Luck's Companion* (New York: Harper and Row, 1979).

Blanche, Ernest E., "Lotteries Yesterday, Today, and Tomorrow," *The Annals of the American Academy of Political and Social Science* 269 (May 1950): 71–76.

Business Week, "Gambling—The Newest Growth Industry" (26 June 1978): 110–111.

Cabot, Anthony N., and Marc H. Rubenstein, "Nevada." In *International Casino Law*, edited by Anthony N. Cabot, William N. Thompson, and Andrew Tottenham, 2d ed. (Reno: Institute for the Study of Gambling, University of Nevada, 1993): 96–103.

Campbell, Felicia, "The Gambling Mystique: A Positive View." Paper presented to the First Annual Conference on Gambling, Las Vegas, Nevada (10 June 1974).

Cassiello, Nicholas, Jr., "New Jersey." In *International Casino Law*, edited by Anthony N. Cabot, William N. Thompson, and Andrew Tottenham, 2d ed. (Reno: Institute for the Study of Gambling, University of Nevada, 1993): 113–129.

Christiansen, Eugene Martin, "Revenues Soar to $30 Billion," *Gaming and Wagering Business* (August–September 1993): 12–35.

Clotfelter, Charles T., and Philip J. Cook, *Selling Hope: State Lotteries in America* (Cambridge, MA: Harvard University Press, 1989).

Cloward, Richard A., and Lloyd E. Ohlin, *Delinquency and Opportunity* (New York: The Free Press of Glencoe, 1960).

Commission on the Review of the National Policy Toward Gambling, *Gambling in America: Appendix 2: Survey of American Gambling Attitudes and Behavior* (Washington, DC: Superintendent of Documents, U.S. Government Printing Office, 1976).

Corporation of the President of The Church of Jesus Christ of Latter Day Saints, *Position of the Church* (Salt Lake City: Corporation of the President of the Church, 1988).

Council of State Governments, *Book of the States 1992–1993* (Lexington, KY: Council of State Governments, 1992): 408–418.

Day, John, "Horse Racing and the Pari-Mutuel," *The Annals of the American Academy of Political and Social Science* 269 (May 1950): 57–58.

Demaris, Ovid, *Boardwalk Jungle* (New York: Bantam Books, 1986).

Dixon, David, "Responses to Illegal Betting in Britain and Australia." In *Gambling Research: Proceedings of the Seventh International Conference on Gambling and Risk Taking*, edited by William R. Eadington, vol. 1. (1988): 247–279.

———, *From Prohibition to Regulation: Bookmaking, Anti-Gambling and the Law* (Oxford: Clarendon Press, 1990).

Dombrink, John, and William N. Thompson, *The Last Resort: Success and Failure in Campaigns for Casinos* (Reno: University of Nevada Press, 1990).

Encyclopedia of Religion, vol. 5. (New York: Scribner, 1928).

Freud, Sigmund, "Dostoyevsky and Parricide." In *Complete Psychological Works of Freud*, edited by James Strachey. (London: Hogarth Press, 1928): 21.

Gaming Control Board (Nevada), *Gaming, Nevada Style* (Carson City: Nevada State Printing Office, 1977).

General Conference of the United Methodist Church, *Social Principles of the United Methodist Church* (Nashville, TN: General Board of Church and Society UMC, 1984).

Grant, Heber J., *Improvement Era* (Salt Lake City: Church of Jesus Christ of the Latter Day Saints, 1926).

Haskins, Jim, *Gambling: Who Really Wins?* (New York: Franklin Watts, 1979).

Hopkins, E. Washburn, *Ethics of India* (Port Washington, NY: Kennikat Press, 1924).

Indian Gaming Regulatory Act of 1988, Public Law 100-497. Passed 25 October 1988.

Jacobs, Louis, *What Does Judaism Say About . . . ?* (New York: Quadrangle, 1973).

Karcher, Alan, *Lotteries* (New Brunswick: Transaction Publications, 1989).

Klein, Howard J., and Gary Selsner, "Results of the First Gallup Organization Study of Legalized Gambling," *Gaming Business Magazine* (November 1982): 5–7, 48–49.

LaFleur, Terri, "A Lottery Grows in Texas: Lone Star Lottery on '92 Ballot," *Gaming and Wagering Business* (September–October 1991): 59.

Lehne, Richard, *Casino Policy* (New Brunswick, NJ: Rutgers University Press, 1986).

Lesieur, Henry, and Robert L. Custer, "Pathological Gambling: Roots, Phases, and Treatment," *Annals of the American Academy of Political and Social Science* 474 (July 1984): 147–148.

Linn, Louis, "Jews and Pathological Gambling." In *Addiction in the Jewish Community*, edited by Stephen Jay Levy. (New York: Commission on Synagogue Relations, 1986): 337–358.

McQueen, Patricia A., "North American Gaming at a Glance," *Gaming and Wagering Business* (September–October 1993): 52–62.

Mangalmurti, Sandeep, and Robert Allan Cooke, *State Lotteries: Seducing the Less Fortunate?*, Heartland Policy Study Number 35. (23 April 1991) (Chicago: The Heartland Institute).

Mikesell, John L., and C. Kurt Zorn, "State Lotteries as Fiscal Savior or Fiscal Fraud," *Public Administration Review* 46 (July–August 1986): 311–320.

Moody, Gordon, Interview with author. London, England. (20 August 1990).

Morgan, Kenneth, *The Path of the Buddha* (New York: The Ronald Press, 1956).

The New Catholic Encyclopedia (New York: McGraw Hill, 1967).

New York Times, 25 February 1992: A-1.

————, 28 February 1992: A-12.

Newman, David, et al., eds., *Esquire's Book of Gambling* (New York: Harper and Row, 1962).

Ochrym, Ronald George, and Clifton Park, "Street Crime, Tourism, and Casinos: An Empirical Comparison" *Journal of Gambling Studies* 6 (Summer 1990): 127–138.

Pelton, R. Wayne, "Laughable Gaming Laws," *Gambling Times,* (Janury 1980): 26–27.

Peterson, Virgil, *Gambling: Should It Be Legalized?* (Springfield, IL: Charles C. Thomas, 1951).

Pollock, Michael, *Hostage to Fortune* (Princeton, NJ: Center for the Analysis of Public Policy, 1987).

Resolution of Central Conference of American Rabbis, 97th Annual Convention, Snowmass, Colorado, 1986.

Rose, I. Nelson, *Gambling and the Law* (North Hollywood, CA: Gambling Times, 1986).

————, "The Legalization and Control of Casino Gambling," *Fordham Law Journal,* vol. 8, no. 2 (1979–1980): 245–300.

Rosecrance, John, *Gambling without Guilt: the Legitimation of an American Pastime* (Pacific Grove, CA: Brooks-Cole, 1988).

Rosenthal, Franz, *Gambling in Islam* (Leiden: Brill, 1975).

Scarne, John, *Scarne's Complete Guide to Gambling* (New York: Simon and Schuster, 1961).

Schacht, Joseph, *An Introduction to Islamic Law* (Oxford: Clarendon Press, 1964).

Smith, James F., "Las Vegas East? Atlantic City Ten Years After the Referendum," *Nevada Public Affairs Review,* Special Issue, no. 2 (1986): 50–55.

Spiro, Melford E., *Buddhism and Society* (Berkeley: University of California Press, 1982).

Starkey, L.M., *Money, Mania, and Morals* (New York: Abington Press, 1964).

Sternlieb, George, and James W. Hughes, *The Atlantic City Gamble* (Cambridge, MA: Harvard University Press, 1983).

Taber, Julian, John L. Collachi, and Edward J. Lynn, "Pathological Gambling: Possibilities for Treatment in Northern Nevada," *Nevada Public Affairs Review*, Special Issue, no. 2 (1986): 39–41.

Thompson, William N., "Machismo: Manifestations of a Cultural Value in the Latin American Casino," *Journal of Gambling Studies* 7 (Summer 1991): 143–164.

———, "The States Bet on Legalized Gambling." In *The 1994 World Book Yearbook* (Chicago: World Book, Inc., 1994): 390–401.

Thompson, William N., and J. Kent Pinney, "The Mismarketing of Dutch Casinos," *Journal of Gambling Studies* 6 (Fall 1990): 205–221.

Time-Life Books, *The Old West: The Gamblers* (Alexandria, VA: Time-Life Books, 1978).

Wagman, Robert, *Instant Millionaires* (Washington, DC: Woodbine House, 1986).

Wayne, Pelton R., "Laughable Gaming Laws," *Gambling Times* (January 1980): 26–27.

Welles, C., "America's Gambling Fever," *Business Week* (24 April 1989): 112–115.

Werblowsky, R. J. Z., and G. Wigoder, eds., *Encyclopedia of the Jewish Religion* (New York: Holt, Rinehart, Winston, 1966).

World Book Encyclopedia, "Buddhism," vol. 2 (Chicago: World Book, Inc., 1978): 555–557.

2

Chronology

THE INSTITUTION OF GAMBLING was well established in North America and throughout the world by the time Captain John Smith brought his colonists to Jamestown in 1607. Almost immediately, Smith was back in London seeking financial help to keep his settlement going. Soon John Smith's Virginia Company was given permission to raise funds through the sale of lottery tickets. The chronology below records critical events in the history of North American gambling from Smith's landing until the 1990s.

1612   A lottery is organized in London to support Virginia Colony in America. Four drawings are held between 1612 and 1615. Ticket purchasers are told they are honoring both "God and Country." Thus are the seeds for modern lottery advertising sown by the founders of the first permanent European settlement on the continent.

1620   Twenty mares are shipped from England to Virginia Colony, and horse racing with private wagering becomes a regular activity for the settlers.

1621   The first restrictions on gambling are established in Plymouth Colony. Opposition to forms of card playing and gambling are also instituted in early Massachusetts Bay Colony. While the lottery activity in London may have saved Virginia Colony, gambling activity is quickly seen as a dangerous vice when taken up by the new settlers, at least in New England. Soon,

1621
cont.
prohibitions on many gambling activities are found throughout the Northeast. The need for these prohibitions serves as an indication that gambling activity is quite widespread among the new Americans from the first days of colonization.

1665
A permanent oval horse racing course is laid out on the Hempstead Plain on Long Island, New York Colony. This marks the commercial beginnings of a facet of the gambling industry in America. Racing before this time consisted of match races over long, straight courses, with betting between individuals only. The new track activity is so successful that soon large oval courses can be found in a majority of the colonies.

1682
The Quaker government of Pennsylvania colony passes anti-gambling legislation. However, the futility of prohibition is witnessed here and elsewhere by continued gambling. Pennsylvania's leading citizen, Benjamin Franklin, is a frequent lottery player throughout his adult life in Philadelphia.

1765
The British Parliament passes the Stamp Act, which provides for the taxation of playing cards. The Act is one of the first of the "Obnoxious Acts" considered responsible for the eventual rebellion in America. That the British target playing cards as a potential source of tax revenues is an indication of how much Americans love card games. A good portion of the card decks found in the colonies at the time were manufactured by America's leading printer, Benjamin Franklin.

1776
Thomas Jefferson gambles as he composes the Declaration of Independence. John Rosecrance's *Gambling without Guilt* describes entries in Jefferson's diary from June 1776, which detail his and his wife's wins and losses at backgammon and lotto. (1988, 18) Following independence, the first wave of legalized gambling manifests as lotteries fund war activities. In 1777, the Continental Congress initiates a lottery game. Massachusetts, New York, and Rhode Island legislative bodies follow suit.

1790s
Lotteries become a major economic tool for financing civic projects. Lottery funds help build the new capital city on the Potomac. Many colleges, including Harvard, Yale, Columbia, Rutgers, and Dartmouth, use lottery monies to construct buildings. Other schools and even churches do the same. From 1790 to 1830, 21 state governments issue licenses for nearly 200 lottery schemes.

1812   The first steamboat operates on the Mississippi River, inaugurating an era of riverboat gambling in the West. The boat is Robert Fulton's "New Orleans." The boat sinks, but is replaced by a larger "New Orleans" in 1815. The new boat has passenger accommodations and spacious areas where card sharks seek to fleece money from farmers and traders.

1815   New Orleans licenses casino gaming enterprises in the city. New Orleans was already wide open to gambling when it became part of the United States with the 1803 Louisiana Purchase. Legislation and licensing are seen as means to control the widespread gambling and generate monies for municipal improvements.

1820   The number of western riverboats with gaming grows to 69.

1827   John Davis opens America's first complete casino in New Orleans at the corner of Orleans and Bourbon Streets. The high-class establishment caters to aristocratic tastes and includes entertainment and the best dining available. Although open only until 1835, it serves as a model for modern Las Vegas and Atlantic City type casinos.

1832   The high point of early lottery play, with 420 lottery games in eight states. However, scandals and mismanagement plague most of the games.

1833   The Jacksonian Era ushers in a mood of general governmental reform. This affects gambling as reformers call for a cessation of all such activity. Pennsylvania and Maryland are the first to prohibit lotteries, and most other states follow suit. Between 1833 and 1840, 12 states ban lotteries. By the time of the Civil War all legal lotteries have halted. This marks the end of the first major wave of legal gambling in America.

1835   New Orleans declares casinos to be illegal. High-class aristocratic gaming halls such as John Davis' close, but lower-class gambling dens continue to operate illegally. The anti-gambling reform movement moves up the Mississippi River. A vigilante committee torches the gambling dens of Vicksburg, Mississippi, and lynches five gamblers.

1848   The gold strike in California marks a new trend: mining camp gambling halls. Eastern reform and western opportunity define the redistribution of gambling sin activity in the 1840s

1848
cont.

and, 100 years later, the 1940s. While opportunity brings prospectors West, reform pushes gamblers in the same direction, with gamblers drawn by the opportunity to strike gold in the halls themselves. San Francisco, the major headquarters for obtaining provisions, becomes a central venue for gambling activity. Much of the San Francisco gaming is concentrated in the Chinese Quarter of the city. Reformers win approval of various anti-gambling laws, but these remain ineffectual as mining continues to attract fortune hunters.

1860

Riverboat gambling reaches its apex, with 557 boats operating on the eve of the Civil War. In *The Old West: The Gamblers*, the editors of Time-Life Books suggest there were as many as 2000 gamblers running games, and it is estimated that 99 percent of them cheated players.

1868

Gambling gets a second wind as the Louisiana Lottery begins a three-decade reign of abuse and corruption. Initially started in order to bring needed revenues to a war-torn, bankrupt state, the lottery is soon overcome by New York entrepreneurs who sustain it by regularly bribing state officials. The lottery enjoys great success as tickets are sold through the mail across the continent.

1887

Charles Fey invents the slot machine in San Francisco. This first machine accepts and pays nickels. Soon similar devices are found throughout the city, and since patents on the concept of a gambling machine are not granted by the government at this time, the door is opened for imitation by other manufacturers. To dodge authorities who declare the machines illegal, manufacturers and operators begin to award merchandise or indirect cash payments to winners. One century after its invention, slot machine gaming will become the number one form of gambling in North American casinos.

1890

Congress bans the sale of lottery tickets through the mail. This significantly affects the Louisiana Lottery, which was the target of the law. Two years later the Louisiana Lottery is voted out of existence. These actions represent the beginning of the end of the second wave of legalized gambling in America.

1891

The Broadmoor Casino Resort opens in Colorado Springs, Colorado. This casino brings a new elegance to Western gaming. The building is 244 feet long and sits beside a lake. As many as 15,000 players visit the establishment each day. How-

1891
cont.

ever, the casino fails to make money from gambling as people gamble among themselves rather than playing "house-banked games," which involve players making wagers against the casino, with the casino always having odds in its favor. The casino is destroyed by fire in 1897.

The first organized regulation of horse racecourses begins with licensing of jockeys and trainers by a private board of control in New York State. The growth in popularity of race betting requires the establishment of integrity in racing, as many bettors were driven away by the fear that races were fixed. Now regulators assure that jockeys, managers, and owners have "clean" backgrounds. Regulators are empowered to ban those caught cheating from racing activities. Track activity is now monitored by neutral parties.

1893
The anti-gambling movement takes hold in Canada as Parliament bans most forms of gambling with revisions to the criminal code.

1894
The Jockey Club of New York is established. It helps to develop national standards for horse racing.

1906
Kentucky becomes the first state to establish a government-run state racing commission. At the same time, other states begin to ban horse racing. Tennessee closes its tracks in 1906; California closes its tracks in 1909; and New York closes its tracks in 1911.

1907
The Arizona and New Mexico Territorial governments outlaw all gambling in their quest for statehood.

1910
The era of anti-gambling reform seems nearly complete. Nevada closes its casinos and legalized gambling in America, with the exception of a few horse race tracks, is dormant.

1931
The state of Nevada legalizes wide-open casino gambling. At first, gaming is confined to small saloons and taverns and is regulated by counties. Casino taxes consist of set fees on each table or machine game. The taxes are shared between local and state governments.

1933
The first totalizator is used at an American horse race track in Arlington Park, Illinois. The totalizator machine allows the track to effectively implement the pari-mutuel system of

1933
cont.
betting (invented in France in 1865). This system permits all bets to be pooled. The track ceases to bet against the players and instead receives a fixed fee or percentage of the betting pool for redistributing the bets from losers to winners. Soon legal horse race betting returns to several Depression-bankrupt (or near bankrupt) states as a revenue mechanism.

1935
New horse-race betting legislation is approved in Illinois, Louisiana, Florida, New Hampshire, West Virginia, Ohio, Michigan, Massachusetts, Rhode Island, and Delaware.

1938
California legalizes horse-race betting.

1940
New York legalizes horse-race betting.

1941
The Las Vegas Strip begins its legacy as the world's primary casino gaming location. The El Rancho Vegas is the first casino on the Strip, and is soon joined by the Last Frontier and the Desert Inn. These new style casinos offer hotel accommodations and recreational amenities to tourists.

1945
Nevada begins to license casinos for the first time. In addition to set fees on games, the casinos begin to pay a tax on the amount of money they win from players. Nevada casino activity increases as World War II ends, but operators of illegal gaming establishments throughout the country face a new wave of reform. Reform is triggered with the end of World War II as public resources and public concern turns to domestic problems. Gamblers shift operations to Las Vegas.

1946
Gangster Benjamin (Bugsy) Siegel, financed by organized crime kingpin Meyer Lansky, opens the Flamingo Casino on the Las Vegas Strip. The casino features a showroom with Hollywood entertainment.

1947
Siegel's murder sensationalizes the Strip and firms up Las Vegas's reputation as a risky, naughty place where main street Americans can rub shoulders with notorious mobsters.

1950
The United States Senate investigates organized crime and gambling casinos. Tennessee Senator Estes Kefauver leads a committee which fingers Las Vegas as a "den of evil" controlled by "the Mob;" his investigations serve mainly to hurry the closure of illegal establishments in other jurisdictions. This hastens their exodus to Las Vegas.

1955   Nevada creates the Gaming Control Board under the direction of the State Treasury Commission. A process of professionalizing gaming regulation begins as an effort to convince federal authorities that the state can run honest, crime-free casinos.

1959   The Nevada Gaming Commission is created to oversee the decisions of the Gaming Control Board. Gaming regulation is removed from the State Treasury Commission.

1963   The third wave of legalized gambling begins with the New Hampshire Lottery. This new sweepstakes is the first government lottery since the closing of the Louisiana Lottery. The state sells its first lottery ticket in 1964. It is a three-dollar ticket for a semiannual game patterned after the Irish Sweepstakes. However, the game does not do as well as the state officials had hoped. Public interest wanes due to the high ticket price and the lengthy wait for lottery results.

1966   Billionaire Howard Hughes moves to Las Vegas and begins to purchase Nevada casinos from owners with suspicious connections to organized crime. This helps to improve the city's image. Hughes has a flamboyant image, but also a reputation as an entrepreneur with integrity. Federal authorities, first led by Attorney General Robert Kennedy, continue to focus attention on organized crime in Nevada.

1967   New York begins a lottery, but it fails to meet state officials' budget expectations. Similar to the New Hampshire games, the lottery's monthly draw game proves to be too slow. Few other jurisdictions take notice of the lottery.

1969   Nevada permits ownership of casinos by public corporations. This action is prompted by the industry's need to maintain and upgrade facilities, and a continuing need to improve the state's image. Howard Hughes stops purchasing casinos under federal antitrust threats, and his disintegration into a complete recluse precludes him from improving his properties. In 1970, he leaves Las Vegas.

New Jersey authorizes a lottery. In 1970 the state begins sales of weekly lottery tickets using mass-marketing techniques. The New Jersey operation is successful from the beginning, and other states realize that large revenues can be gained from gaming if ticket prices are low and games occur regularly. Lotteries begin to spread quickly.

1969
cont. The Canadian Penal Code is amended to permit government lotteries and charity gaming. Soon all the provinces have lotteries, and the door is opened for charities and governments to offer casino games.

1970 The Yukon Territory permits the Klondike Visitor's Association to conduct casino games from mid-spring through the summer at Diamond Tooth Gerties in Dawson City.

Lotto Quebec, an agency of the Quebec provincial government, initiates the first lottery gaming in Canada.

1974 Massachusetts becomes the first North American jurisdiction to introduce an instant lottery game. This becomes the most popular lottery game of the decade, and all other lotteries begin to sell instant games.

The Western Canada Lottery Corporation initiates the first intergovernmental lottery in North America. The provinces of Manitoba, Saskatchewan, Alberta, and British Columbia operate these games together. British Columbia later drops out of the joint operation in order to have its own lottery games.

1975 New Jersey starts the first "numbers game" with players selecting their own three-digit numbers. The game is offered with hopes that it will drive the popular illegal numbers games out of business. Other lotteries adopt the numbers game as well, often adding a four-digit number game. There is little evidence that illegal games will stop.

1975–1976 The Commission on the Review of the National Policy Toward Gambling issues a report affirming the notion that gambling activity—its legalization and control—is a matter for the jurisdictions of state governments. The commission is authorized by the 1970 Organized Crime Control Act.

1976 New Jersey voters authorize casino gambling for Atlantic City by a margin of 56 percent to 44 percent. The successful 1976 campaign follows an unsuccessful campaign for casinos in 1974. The campaign is well financed by the Resorts International Casino organization of the Bahamas. Minor opposition by religious officials is unorganized.

1977 New Jersey creates a regulatory structure for casino gaming which includes the independent Casino Control Commission

1977
cont.
and the Division of Gaming Enforcement within the state attorney general's office.

1978
Casino gaming begins in Atlantic City with the opening of Resorts International. Crowds jam the single casino, which realizes windfall profits from a monopoly status that lasts 14 months.

High-stakes bingo games begin on the Seminole Indian reservation in Hollywood, Florida, signaling a new period of Indian gambling. In subsequent federal court litigation, the Indians retain the right to conduct games that are unregulated by the state.

The Province of Ontario initiates the world's first lotto game, called "Lottario." The game requires players to select six numbers and all play is entered into an online computer network. A jackpot prize is given to any player that picks all six numbers. If there is no winner, more prize money is added to the next drawing.

Jackpots in American lotto games have grown to exceed $100 million. Soon afterwards, Quebec introduces its own on-line lotto game. Many states and provinces rush to imitate the lotto games, which quickly lead all other types of lottery games in sales.

1985
The Canadian national government agrees to place responsibility for the administration of all gambling laws with the provinces in exchange for a $100-million payment to offset the costs of Calgary Winter Olympics of 1988. The penal code is revised in accordance with the agreement.

1985–
1986
The President's Commission on Organized Crime fails to issue a report on gambling, as it now considers gambling to be, for the most part, a legitimate industry.

1987
The United States Supreme Court upholds the rights of Indian tribes to offer unregulated gambling enterprises as long as operations do not violate state criminal policy. The case *Cabazon v. California* determines that any regulation of non-criminal matters must come from the federal government or be specifically authorized by Congress.

1988
The Indian Gaming Regulatory Act is passed by Congress in response to the Cabazon decision. The act provides for federal

1988
cont.

and tribal regulation of bingo games, and for mutually negoti-ated Indian-state government schemes for the regulation of casinos on reservations.

The voters of South Dakota authorize limited ($5) stakes casino games of blackjack, poker, and slot machines in casinos in the historic town of Deadwood.

1989

The South Dakota legislature passes enabling laws and gaming begins in Deadwood. The gaming is regulated by the South Dakota Commission on Gaming. A state lottery also begins operation of video lottery terminals throughout South Dakota.

The Iowa state legislature approves riverboat casino gam-ing with limited ($5) stakes betting on navigable waters in the state. The State of Oregon starts the first sports game-based lottery in the United States. Prizes are given to players who select four out of four winners of football or basketball games. Point spread handicaps are utilized. Proceeds of the gambling are assigned to support college athletics in Oregon. Still, University of Oregon and Oregon State University teams re-main mired near the bottom of all Pacific Ten Conference standings. It is perceived that gambling enterprise can only contribute so much.

The Manitoba Lottery Foundation, a government-owned en-tity, opens the first year-round permanent casino facility in Canada. The Crystal Casino is located in the classic Fort Garry Hotel in Winnipeg.

The jackpot prize in the Pennsylvania lotto game exceeds $115 million. It is won, and shared, by several lucky ticket holders.

1990

Riverboat casinos begin operation in Iowa. Riverboat casinos are also approved by the Illinois state legislature. The voters of Colorado approve limited casino gaming for the historic mountain towns of Blackhawk, Cripple Creek, and Central City.

1991

Riverboat casinos are approved by the Mississippi legislature. It is determined that the boats may be permanently docked.

Oregon and Colorado introduce keno as a lottery game.

1992   The Atlantic Provinces—New Brunswick, Prince Edward's Island, Nova Scotia, and Newfoundland—authorize video lottery terminals for locations throughout their territories.

The Louisiana legislature approves riverboat casinos and one land-based casino in New Orleans. Missouri voters also approve riverboat casinos.

Congress prohibits the spread of sports betting beyond four states currently authorizing it: Nevada, Oregon, Montana, and Delaware. New Jersey is given one year to approve sports betting for an Atlantic City casino, but the state declines to do so.

1993   The Ontario government approves a casino for the city of Windsor. The casino is to be government owned but privately operated. The Provincial government selects a consortium of Las Vegas casino companies, including Caesars Palace, Circus Circus, and the Hilton, to operate the casino. The Province of Quebec opens a government-owned and operated casino in Montreal at the site of the French Pavilion of the Montreal World's Fair.

The Indiana legislature approves boat casinos. Five boats are authorized for Lake Michigan ports, five for ports on the Ohio River, and one for an interior lake.

3

Biographical Sketches

GAMBLING HAS AT SOME POINT been embraced in every society, and some may feel these activities are directed by forces above and beyond the control of mortals. This would be an erroneous belief.

The gambling industry today responds to social forces, to be sure. But these responses have catalysts. The catalytic forces are manifest in individuals who see opportunities to be exploited, or who perhaps see an emerging phenomenon that requires controls. It has been this way through the ages as players, entrepreneurs, and government leaders responded in different ways to a universal activity. This section is not comprehensive, but rather presents representative profiles of persons in North America who have demonstrated an impact on the gaming industry. Indeed, with the rapid growth that has been witnessed, new industry giants may spring up to map the direction of gambling in the future.

The first section includes individuals who have been inducted into *International Gaming and Wagering Business'* Gambling Hall of Fame since its inception in 1989. The second section lists leading entrepreneurs who have guided the development of the industry, while the third group consists of top players in the history of gambling. All of these personalities have helped to shape the gaming industry into its current form.

Gambling Hall of Fame

John Ascuaga

Born in Caldwell, Idaho in 1926, John Ascuaga graduated from Washington State University and began working in gaming resorts in Idaho. However, when Idaho enforced the banning of slot machines in 1953, Ascuaga moved to Nevada. He worked with Richard Graves, an entrepreneur who had owned Idaho resorts. Ascuaga managed Graves' properties in both Carson City and Sparks, Nevada. In 1960 he purchased the Sparks Nugget—now called Ascauga's Nugget. Ascuaga developed the property into one of the leading privately owned casino hotel resorts in Nevada. John Ascuaga has also been a leading citizen, sponsoring a college education fund for top high-school students in the state of Nevada.

William Bennett

Born in 1925 in Glendale, Arizona, Bill Bennett came to Las Vegas in 1966 as executive vice president of Del Webb's Mint Hotel and Casino. In 1974 he purchased the Circus Circus property in partnership with Bill Pennington. The two entrepreneurs developed Circus Circus Enterprises into the best "return on investment" gaming properties in the world. Their flagship casino, the Luxor, and the 4,000 room Excalibur are located in Las Vegas. The company also owns casinos in Laughlin and Reno, Nevada.

Benny Binion

Born in Texas in 1904, Benny Binion ran poker games and numbers in his native state until relocating to Las Vegas in 1946. He quickly became a legend in his new hometown by developing the Horseshoe Casino, a property that catered to high-rolling professional gamblers. Binion accepted bets without limits. He founded the World Championship of Poker, held each year at the Horseshoe Casino. The "cowboy gambler" died in 1989.

Sam Boyd

Born in Oklahoma in 1910, Sam Boyd came to Las Vegas in 1941 after running bingo parlors in Hawaii. He worked in the local casinos for several years before developing a number of properties, including the Union Plaza, California Hotel, and Sam's Town. Boyd became one of gaming's most successful entrepreneurs before his death in 1992.

William S. Boyd

After practicing law for 15 years, William S. Boyd joined his father, Sam, in the 1970s to launch a group of casinos under the family name. Today he serves as the chief executive officer and chairman for operations in Las Vegas and Clark counties, and also has planned new ventures for Louisiana.

James Crosby

A businessman and developer, James Crosby was instrumental in the remake of Atlantic City as the gambling mecca of the eastern United States. In the 1950s he participated in a stock takeover of the Mary Carter Paint Company. To diversify, the company purchased a land development operation in the Bahamas in the early 1960s. Following soon after this was the purchase of the Bahamas' Paradise Island Casino resort. From this base, Crosby was able to influence New Jersey politicians and voters on casino legalization. His company, now called Resorts International, opened the first Atlantic City casino in 1978.

Jackie Gaughan

A Las Vegas casino entrepreneur, Jackie Gaughan was born and raised in Omaha, Nebraska. He is credited with much of the development that has resulted in downtown Las Vegas making a major contribution to the modern casino scene. His properties include the Union Plaza and the El Cortez.

Henry Gluck

Born in Germany, Henry Gluck came to the United States in 1936. He attended Wharton School of Finance and eventually advanced to the vice presidency of Monogram Industries. He retired at the age of 43. In the early 1970s, Gluck returned to the corporate scene as the chairman of Caesars World. He succeeded in resuscitating the slipping Caesars Palace and restoring it as an industry giant.

Harvey Gross

Entering the casino business with six stools and slot machines at a Lake Tahoe gambling house in 1944, Harvey Gross's property has grown into Harvey's Resort Hotel and Casino, a leader in the northern Nevada gaming industry. Today, the property boasts 88,000 square feet of gaming space and a 740-room hotel. With Gross's leadership, Lake Tahoe has become a vital casino resort destination. Harvey Gross died in 1983.

William F. Harrah

A native of California, Bill Harrah was born in 1911. He brought his Golden State bingo hall experience to Reno in the late 1930s. Over four decades he built the Harrah's gambling empire around the concept of servicing the small player. Harrah was the first casino operator to utilize tour buses for players, and transported customers between his properties in central and northern California and the casinos he operated in Reno and Lake Tahoe. His was among the first gaming companies to be publicly traded on national stock exchanges. Harrah died in 1978.

Barron Hilton

The second son of Conrad Hilton was born in 1927. After several independent business ventures, he joined the Hilton Hotel Corporation in the 1950s. He made his mark with the company by guiding it into the gambling business. Soon after Nevada permitted public corporations to own casinos, Hilton acquired the Las Vegas International Hotel and Casino, at that time the largest hotel in the world. Hilton also purchased the Flamingo Casino on the Las Vegas Strip, as well as gaming properties in Reno and Laughlin, Nevada. The Hilton Corporation's profits from its Nevada gaming properties exceed its profits from all its other American properties combined. Barron Hilton has considerable interests outside gaming as well. He was the founding owner of the Los Angeles Chargers (now the San Diego Chargers).

Kirk Kerkorian

Born in Fresno, California in 1917, Kirk Kerkorian, like Howard Hughes, was an airline executive before developing an attraction to casino ventures in Las Vegas. Kerkorian is responsible for the development of some of the largest resorts in the gaming industry. His first project was the International, now called the Las Vegas Hilton. Next was the MGM Grand, which is now owned by Bally's. Each was the largest hotel in the world when it opened. In 1993 he opened the new MGM Grand on the Strip. The new Grand is now the largest hotel in the world with 5,000 rooms. It sits beside a movie land theme park.

Sol Kerzner

The legendary founding force behind Sun International's massive casino empire in southern Africa, Sol Kerzner pioneered the notion of developing a mega-resort around gaming when he developed Sun City in 1978. His idea of an entirely self-contained resort complex with a hotel, recreation, and entertainment became the benchmark for American casino developers who followed a decade later.

Don Laughlin

Growing up in Owantonne, Minnesota, during the 1940s, as a child Don Laughlin became fascinated with intricate machinery— especially slot machines. He purchased a slot machine through a mail-order catalogue and arranged to have it placed in a local VFW Club. He used the profits from the machine to buy another, then another. Soon he was expelled from high school because the principal did not like the fact that Laughlin's illegal gambling earnings exceeded his own salary. Minnesota authorities were very lax about enforcing gaming laws until the federal government passed the Sullivan Act in 1950. A crackdown ensued, and it became impossible to get new slot machines shipped into the state. Laughlin moved to Las Vegas in 1952, and two years later he owned a small bar and casino. For ten years he ground out profits and saved for a bigger investment. That investment turned out to be a run-down motel and casino on the Arizona border at the southernmost point of Nevada, 90 miles south of Las Vegas. Laughlin prospered by catering to drive-in visitors from Arizona and California, especially senior citizens who wintered in the Southwest. With Laughlin's vision, a new gaming town—Laughlin, Nevada—grew. Today it boasts many large casinos, including a Hilton, a Golden Nugget, and a Circus Circus. Some of these properties have upwards of 2,000 hotel rooms.

Warren Nelson

Born in Great Falls, Montana, in 1913, Warren Nelson started a 45-year gaming career in the Big Sky State, which quickly led him to Reno, Nevada. Nelson came to Reno in 1936 to work at the Palace Club. He is responsible for bringing Keno into the casinos for the first time. During World War II Nelson served in the Marines, but he returned to Reno afterwards. In the early 1960s he purchased the Cal-Neva Club in Reno; he later bought the Comstock in Reno. Nelson also held interests in Las Vegas casinos. Among gaming pioneers, he was a leader who was able to attract people before the national marketing days of modern corporate Nevada.

Donald (Mike) O'Callaghan

From 1971 to 1979, Mike O'Callaghan served as governor of Nevada. This was a period of incredible casino expansion, as O'Callaghan assumed office just as the state began to allow corporate ownership of casinos. O'Callaghan was born in La Crosse, Wisconsin, in 1929, was a decorated Korean War veteran, and came to Nevada as a school teacher. He held many administrative posts that finally led to the governorship of the state. As governor he helped guide major companies like Hilton and MGM into casino gaming. O'Callaghan established the Gaming Policy Committee and helped the state adjust its policies in the face of new competition from Atlantic City. Following his two terms as governor, he became managing editor of the *Las Vegas Sun*.

Bill Pennington

Born in 1923, Bill Pennington spent many years in the Las Vegas casino industry running slot route operations before teaming up with William Bennett in 1974. The two men pooled $40,000 in savings and purchased the Circus Circus casino on the Las Vegas Strip at a time when the operation was on the verge of bankruptcy. The two men reorganized operations and focused the property with a family orientation. Their success was phenomenal. They later expanded into Reno and Laughlin, as well as developing other new mega-resorts in Las Vegas. Pennington suffered major injuries in a boat accident in 1984 and his business involvement with Circus Circus subsided. He retired as chief executive officer in 1988, but remains active on the board of directors.

Leonard Prescott

In the space of ten years, Leonard Prescott rose from the position of manual laborer on the Shakopee Mdewakanton Dakota reservation in Minnesota to that of recognized leader of Indian gaming in America. In 1987 he became tribal chairman, and in 1991, chief executive officer of the Tribes Little Six gaming property. He was a founding member of the National Indian Gaming Association.

Si Redd

The "Emperor of Slots" was born in Philadelphia, Mississippi in 1911. For many years he was a slot machine distributor for Bally's Gaming. In the 1970s he developed the video gaming machine and independently started his own production with a company that became International Gaming Technologies. IGT is the leading slot machine company in the world today.

Jay Sarno

Jay Sarno was born in 1921 in St. Joseph, Missouri. He attended the University of Missouri before venturing to Nevada after World War II. Sarno introduced the idea of a theme-based casino resort to the stagnating gambling industry of the 1960s. He built Caesars Palace and operated it from 1966 to 1969. The notion that a casino could be developed around a central idea, such as life in ancient Rome, was novel, and gave Las Vegas a boost of marketing publicity that was missing at a time when Howard Hughes was accumulating and, in effect, "warehousing" properties. Sarno's vision expanded when he moved north on the Strip and created Circus Circus. Although Sarno did not experience the tremendous profits these properties later realized, his role was essential in the success of not only Caesars and Circus Circus, but of Las Vegas itself during recent years. Sarno died in 1984.

Grant Sawyer

Born in Idaho in 1918, Grant Sawyer graduated from the University of Nevada in 1941. After service with the infantry in World War II, Sawyer completed studies at George Washington University Law School. He began practicing law in Elko, Nevada. Sawyer was active in politics and graduated from the position of Elko

County district attorney to that of governor in 1958. He served two terms, leaving the office at the end of 1966. During his tenure Sawyer directed the restructuring of casino regulation in the state. Under his leadership, the state maintained its independence in gaming regulation. Attorney General Robert Kennedy attempted to transfer regulatory functions to federal authorities, but Sawyer's negotiating skills prevented this from occurring. In his last year as governor, Sawyer was influential in persuading billionaire Howard Hughes to take over several Las Vegas casinos which had troubled ownerships and were therefore more susceptible to federal investigations. Sawyer later entered law as a successful partner in one of the world's leading gaming law firms: Lionel, Sawyer, and Collins of Las Vegas.

Raymond Smith

"Pappy" Smith was a California carnival game operator before coming to Reno and opening Harold's Club in 1937. Smith popularized casino gaming by offering lower stakes games (penny roulette), bright signs, and clean facilities. He also made Nevada gaming an item of nationwide discussion by erecting more than 2,000 highway billboards across the country which proclaimed his motto: "Harold's Club or Bust."

E. Parry Thomas

Born and educated in Utah, Thomas came to Las Vegas in the 1950s. He founded the Bank of Las Vegas (later called the Valley Bank and now part of the Bank of America) and provided loans for casino development in the 1950s and 1960s. This was a time when banks generally refused to advance funds for gaming operations. Thomas has been called "the most powerful prime mover in Las Vegas" by author Mario Puzo.

Claudine Williams

Growing up in De Soto Parish, Louisiana, as a teenager Claudine Williams took a job in a restaurant bar that offered gaming to help her family. She was fascinated by the games and she set about to learn as much as she could. Soon she had saved enough money to go into the business. At the age of 19, she opened the Bonita Club in Galveston, Texas. The operation was successful for several years, as Texas authorities were reluctant to enforce gaming laws.

But in the 1960s the attitudes of Texas officials changed and Williams moved to Las Vegas with her husband, who was also employed in the industry. Years of hard work and saving resulted in Williams' investment in a new casino, the Riverboat, which opened on the Strip in 1972. The Riverboat flourished and grew. It became the Holiday Casino in 1983, and, with further growth, the largest Holiday Inn in the world. Later Williams sold the property to the Holiday Corporation, which in turn was taken over by Harrah's.

Steve Wynn

A New York native, Steve Wynn was born in 1942. After graduating from the University of Pennsylvania, he took over a family bingo operation in Maryland. He came to Las Vegas in 1966 and got involved in several business ventures. In the early 1970s, he was able to parlay a land purchase from Howard Hughes and its subsequent resale into the capital necessary for a substantial investment in the Golden Nugget. Soon he gained a seat on the Nugget's corporate board, and used the position to win control of the operation. Under Wynn's leadership, the Golden Nugget become a leading player in the casino industry, acquiring first a New Jersey property and, later, building the Mirage on the Las Vegas Strip—one of the most profitable and glamorous megaresorts in the world.

Operators and Investors

Richard Canfield

Described in *The Encyclopedia of Gambling* as the most successful gambler America ever produced, Richard Canfield, as with other casino owners, would have denied that he was a gambler, knowing that the odds were always in his favor. Born in New Bedford, Massachusetts, in 1855, he began working as a teenager in seaside gaming resorts. By age 18 he had learned enough to take control of operations at a Providence, Rhode Island, poker hall. Then he set about learning the trade by visiting the leading casinos of Europe. With his new knowledge he returned to America, established illegal casinos in a series of towns, and later set up shop in New York City. Canfield ran the Big Apple's most exclusive casino during the 1880s and 1890s. In 1902, he opened another exclusive gaming hall in Saratoga, New York. There, he ran very high-stakes games, especially during the racing season at the local track. When reform politicians won office, Canfield was finally forced to close doors in 1907. He devoted the final years of his life to philanthropy and art collection and died in 1914.

Morris Bernard (Moe) Dalitz

Moe Dalitz was born in Detroit in 1908. He was active in many businesses in Michigan and Ohio in the 1920s and 1930s. Dalitz allegedly played a role in Midwest bootlegging operations during Prohibition. He came to Las Vegas in the late 1940s and arranged the financing of the Desert Inn Casino Resort. Dalitz is considered to be the man responsible for developing much of the glamour image, as well as the growth, of Las Vegas. He brought headliner entertainment to the casinos, and also championship golf. Additionally, Dalitz developed housing projects and a major hospital and shopping center. He died in Las Vegas in 1989.

John Davis

The *Encyclopedia of Gambling* has described John Davis as "America's First Casino Operator." In 1827, he opened a casino on Bourbon Street in the French Quarter of New Orleans. His 24-hour establishment offered luxurious amenities to the aristocratic players of the day. Davis served the finest French wines, food, and cigars in a style that today is reserved for the highest-rolling casino players. Competing gambling dens in New Orleans and in other riverside towns were down-market dives in comparison. Davis' establishment operated until reformers succeeded in prohibiting casino gambling in the Cresent City in 1835.

Howard Robard Hughes

A leading entrepreneur of twentieth-century America, Howard Hughes was born in 1905. In the 1930s and 1940s, he gained fame as an aviator and a movie producer. He was the major owner of Trans World Airlines, but was forced to sell his stock in an antitrust action in 1966. He used the proceeds from the sale in an attempt to gain control over casino gaming on the Las Vegas Strip. At one time Hughes owned a third of the Strip's casinos. His investments have been credited with lending an aura of legitimacy to casino gaming. Hughes died in 1976.

John North

A disreputable character who specialized in crooked gambling, John North worked as the boss of gambling dens in Vicksburg, Mississippi, during the 1820s and 1830s. Many people lost fortunes as a result of his dishonest operations. A group of local vigilantes organized against the gamblers. After exposing a plot by North to take control of all criminal activity from Vicksburg to New Orleans in 1835, they burned down Vicksburg's riverfront gambling halls and executed dozens of operators and players. North escaped, but was soon captured by the vigilantees and hanged with a roulette wheel tied to his body.

Jim O'Leary

On 8 October 1871, 18-year-old Louis M. Cohn was shooting craps in a barn owned by the O'Learys. His memoirs indicate that his dice-throwing hand accidentally upset a lantern, which ignited some hay, spread, and burned the city of Chicago. The O'Learys, seeking an alibi, came up with the story of an unruly cow kicking over the lantern. The O'Learys' son, Jim, spent his formative years training in the gambling tradition and later opened gambling houses in and around Chicago. In 1904 he operated a gambling boat on Lake Michigan. O'Leary specialized in horse-race bookmaking in addition to bets on other sporting events and election results. By the time he died in 1926 he was a multimillionaire.

Edward Pendleton

The nation's capital city has a long history of vice and corruption. Edward Pendleton occupies more than a footnote in this history. In 1832 he opened Pendleton's Palace, a gambling hall that catered to the empowered elite of society. Congressmen, cabinet members, and even President James Buchanan sat at Pendleton's tables. Prior to the Civil War, this gambling arena was declared neutral territory between the emerging Blue and Gray factions. As politicians became indebted to Pendleton, he began to wield considerable political influence and was able to assist in the passage of many bills concerned with private interests. Several leading

Democrats were pallbearers at his funeral in 1858, and some of the most powerful figures in the country found themselves relieved that Pendleton's IOU.s would not be collected.

Stuart and Clifford Perlman

The Perlman brothers set up a small Miami restaurant specializing in hot dogs in 1956. By the late 1960s their venture had evolved into Lums, Inc., a restaurant chain with 379 outlets. In 1969 the profitable company purchased the Caesars Palace Casino and Hotel in Las Vegas. Under the Perlman's guidance, Caesars became the premier casino in the world. They expanded this domain into Lake Tahoe and Atlantic City. However, the Perlmans were unable to win a license to operate the casino in New Jersey, and in 1981 they left the corporation.

Benjamin Siegel

Popularly known as the "man who invented Las Vegas," nicknamed "Bugsy" (but never to his face), Siegel grew up in New York neighborhoods controlled by mobsters. At an early age he became an associate of Meyer Lansky and the two launched a lifelong partnership in organized crime. Lansky became the financial master behind organized crime ventures across America and the Western world. Siegel's life with the Mob led to liaisons with leading Hollywood moguls and movie stars. He launched many illegal gaming operations from his Los Angeles base, and developed the notion that a desert casino on the outskirts of Las Vegas could attract the movie industry crowd and the globe's most glamorous jet setters. Siegel shepherded the construction and early operations of the Flamingo, then the world's most luxurious casino, and Lansky organized financing for the venture, which opened during the Christmas holidays of 1946. However, Lansky discovered that Siegel had been siphoning casino investment funds into his private accounts, and in June of 1947 Siegel was murdered in the apartment of his actress girlfriend. The murder sensationalized the Las Vegas casino industry and gave the city a reputation as a place of daring adventure. If Siegel didn't invent Las Vegas, his death certainly put it on the map.

Donald Trump

Born in Queens, New York, in 1946, Donald Trump graduated from the Wharton School of Finance at the University of Pennsylvania in 1968 and later worked with his father's construction and apartment management firm. During the 1970s and early 1980s, Trump was instrumental in developing several New York hotels, as well as Trump Tower, the tallest and most expensive reinforced concrete structure in New York City. In the mid-1980s Trump's attention turned to Atlantic City, where he built the Trump Plaza, Trump Castle, and the Taj Mahal. At its opening in 1989, the Taj Mahal was the largest and highest-volume casino in the world. In the 1990s Trump had become firmly entrenched as the leading entrepreneurial force in the Atlantic City gaming market.

Del Webb

Born in Fresno, California, in 1899, Del Webb was a high school dropout who became a professional baseball player in the 1920s. After his short athletic career he started a construction business which grew to become one of the largest in the world. Among other accomplishments, his firm build Sun City in Arizona. Construction profits allowed Webb to re-enter the sports world. In 1945 he purchased one-half interest in the New York Yankees. Webb owned the team during its glory days and sold out to CBS in 1965. In 1946, Webb's company built the Flamingo Hotel and Casino for Benjamin Siegel. He also built a number of other Las Vegas casinos, including the Mint and the Sahara, which were constructed for two friends. When Webb's friends could no longer maintain the properties, Webb created a private dummy corporation in 1961 and purchased the two casinos. Webb soon expanded his gambling interests to Reno, Lake Tahoe, and Atlantic City. He was a major industry player until his death in 1974.

Famous Players

Nicholas Andreas Dandolos

The legendary Nicholas Dandolos is known for having won as much as $50 million in a single evening of play. Yet he also experienced losses just as sizable. Dandolos played this rags-to-riches scenario repeatedly during his life and was popularly known as "Nick the Greek." Dandolos was born on the Greek island of Crete in 1893 and migrated to America at age 18. His gambling activity started with horse tracks in Montreal. He soon earned a reputation across America and became an essential fixture on the Las Vegas scene as Nevada casinos expanded. His exploits were well publicized by casinos seeking notoriety. The James Bond movie *Goldfinger* incorporated schemes developed by Nick the Greek. Known as a great philanthropist, Dandolos donated millions to charities throughout his gaming years. He died on Christmas Day, 1966.

George Devol

Considered the most talented of the riverboat gamblers, George Devol was born in 1829. He started gambling quite early as a ten-year-old cabin boy, and developed cheating techniques that won him more than $2 million over a 40-year career on riverboats and in mining camp saloons and casinos. His favorite schemes involved the game of three-card monte. Devol's escapades are recorded in his autobiography, *40 Years a Gambler on the Mississippi*, published in 1892. Devol reformed in his later years, gave speeches that condemned gambling, and lived a quiet life until his death in 1902.

Alice Duffield

Affectionately known as "Poker Alice," Alice Duffield was born in England during the 1850s. She ventured to America at the age of 12. Although educated in a fashionable southern school, Duffield lost all her sophistication when she moved west. Following the death of her husband she taught school, but Duffield found her true calling as a poker player in the saloons of Colorado and other Western locales. Her rough and rowdy ways featured a cigar profile, foul mouth, and quick action with a gun. Her final gambling post was in Fort Meade, South Dakota, which operated until reform politicians closed it down in 1920. Thereafter, Poker Alice retired to reminisce and smoke cigars until her death in 1930.

John W. Gates

John W. "Bet A Million" Gates was known to have gambled thousands of dollars on events such as the direction of the next train on a track, the speed of a raindrop running down a window pane, or the number of flies to land on a piece of bread. The inveterate risk taker was born in 1855. However, prior to making gambling his avocation, he amassed a great fortune as a manufacturer of barbed wire. With his substantial bankroll, Gates wagered continuously, winning big and losing big. Gates earned his nickname when he attempted to place a million dollar bet on a single horse in a race. The bookies refused to cover his action as the wager was made prior to the days of pari-mutuel betting. Gates maintained his business career during his gambling years and was one of the early investors in U.S. Steel. He died in 1911.

James Butler Hickok

The legendary "Wild Bill" Hickok was a lawman, gunman, and notoriously poor poker player. He was born in 1837 and learned to survive as a gambler only through intimidation. Often he persuaded winners to leave their money on the table with threats of a gunfight. His prowess with a gun usually was not challenged. However, while playing poker in Deadwood, South Dakota's Saloon Number 10 on 2 August 1876, he was shot in the back of the head. Hickok was holding a pair of aces and a pair of eights, a combination that came to be known as "The Dead Man's Hand." It is alleged that his murderer, Jack McCall, had been cheated out of a winning hand earlier by the bullying Hickok.

George Rickard

"Tex" Rickard was born in Kansas City, Missouri. By the age of 23 he was a town marshall in Texas, spending all his leisure time in the gambling halls. The lure of the Yukon Gold Rush beckoned him north to new gambling opportunities. Rickard invested his winnings in a Dawson City saloon called the Monte Carlo, but lost the property in a card game. He returned to the States to become a major boxing promoter and staged fights in New York City and Nevada. When he died in 1929, Rickard was lauded for his reputation as an honest player.

Arnold Rothstein

Born in New York in 1882, Arnold Rothstein became the most widely known gambler in the country and left several marks on the gaming industry. He was a high-stakes player. Rothstein is also credited with being an initial organizer of Prohibition-era crime. He worked with the young Meyer Lansky and Lucky Luciano during their nascent criminal stages. Rothstein ran several New York gaming establishments through the 1920s. In 1919 he was reportedly involved in a sports betting operation that fixed the World Series. He or his confederates were able to bribe several members of the Chicago White Sox to lose some series games. Supposedly, Rothstein earned $270,000 by betting against the Sox. Rothstein was murdered in 1928 in a New York City poker game.

John Scarne

Born in 1903, John Scarne became fascinated with cards in his pre-teen years. But his passion was directed somewhat differently than that of other gamblers. Scarne sought to discover how other gamblers made crooked moves and then developed methods to expose these players. While he was a gambler himself, his career was devoted to ensuring the honesty of gaming contests. Scarne became an advisor to the FBI and other police agencies, as well as to casinos. In an effort to help servicemen avoid being cheated, he advised the United States Army during the Second World War. Scarne left his mark on the industry with the publication of several comprehensive books on gambling rules. He died in 1985.

Alvin Clarence Thomas

Known as "Titanic Thompson," Alvin Thomas was "the king of the proposition bet." Born in poverty, he entertained himself as a child by inventing competitive games and mastering the skills necessary to win. He would place bets on shooting at targets, throwing rocks, cards, dice, golf, horse races, or anything else available at the moment. Thomas invariably won the game at hand. His nickname came from an exhausted opponent, who exclaimed, "You must be Titanic, you sink everybody." During the Depression, Thompson was recognized along with Nick the Greek as being one of the most cunning gamblers in America.

Kenneth S. Uston

The man who popularized the practice of "counting cards" at blackjack games, Ken Uston was trained as a stockbroker and held degrees from both Yale and Harvard. But in the 1960s he learned of the method by which a player could track the cards already dealt in blackjack and project the remaining odds that future combinations would be dealt. When there was a high probability that a natural blackjack (one ace and one ten or face card) would be dealt, the deck favored the player. This is because the house will pay a player $3 for each $2 wager ($3 plus the $2) when a natural blackjack falls. However, losing means the player only loses $2, regardless of the cards held by the house dealer. Uston perfected counting techniques and wrote over a dozen books for blackjack players. He also gave classes for would-be players. As a result of his skilled play, Uston won considerable sums of money at blackjack tables. He was subsequently banned from casino play. He resorted to using disguises and also brought legal action against casinos. Uston won court rulings in New Jersey that forced casinos to open their doors to him. However, his court actions in Nevada were not successful. New Jersey casinos adjusted to the fact they had to let "counters" play by altering their rules and shuffling decks more frequently. Actually, Uston helped the casinos by popularizing the game. He inspired many players with false hopes that they could beat the house. As a result of the card-counting movement, blackjack is now the most popular table game in American casinos. Uston died in Paris while working on a computer investment project.

Rudolph W. Wanderone

Known as "Minnesota Fats," Rudolph W. Wanderone gained fame under the nickname. He was born in 1913, was an expert at pool and billiards by the time he entered grade school, and became an expert hustler. With a 51-inch waist, Fats considered himself the "World's Greatest Athletic." His persona was the model for the pool player portrayed by Jackie Gleason in the 1961 classic film *The Hustler.*

4

Legislation, Points of View, and Statistics

THE STATUTES AND CASES INCLUDED in this chapter have been selected as representative of major policy developments in the gaming field. Because legalized gambling was not widely prevalent and there were few laws and cases until the latter half of the twentieth century in the United States and Canada, the majority of legislation in this section is from this period.

As the law continues to evolve, new jurisdictions are entering legalization phases, and old questions addressed by judges—such as responsibility for compulsive gambling—are taking on new meaning as gambling is now widespread across the continent. The synopses of laws and cases are not presented as professional legal opinions regarding the law, but rather as a starting point for further research.

National statutory laws in the United States and Canada are presented in chronological order. Selected state and provincial legislation and orders are presented in alphabetical order of jurisdictions. Law cases appear in chronological order.

The laws and cases reviewed in this chapter are rich with statements on the nature of the gambling industry and the gambling phenomenon. The Points of View section contains specific passages from this body of information as well as passages from other sources. An attempt has been made to present viewpoints both favorable to and critical of the gambling industry.

U.S. Federal Gaming Legislation

The United States Congress has enacted many laws pertaining to gambling. Most have dealt with lotteries and interstate commerce; however, in recent years attention has been given to casino gambling on Indian reservations and on ships at sea.

Flower Garden Banks National Marine Sanctuary
(Public Law 102-251, 9 March 1992)

This act amends the Gambling Devices Act (Johnson Act) by permitting gambling on ships carrying the American flag, but only if they do so outside the waters of a state, or with the permission of a state. A state may refuse to allow such a ship to dock unless the ship also docks in a foreign port. This act basically reversed an act of 1948 which prohibited gambling on American ships.

Professional and Amateur Sports Protection Act
(Public Law 102-559, 28 October 1992)

This act prohibits betting on sports events throughout the nation, with the exception of wagering in the casinos of Nevada and in the Oregon sports lottery. Limited sports betting was also allowed to continue in Montana and Delaware. New Jersey was given the option of having sports betting in Atlantic City casinos if it authorized the betting before the end of 1993. New Jersey failed to do so.

Indian Gaming Regulatory Act of 1988
(Public Law 100-497, 25 October 1988)

This law established a framework for regulating gambling activities on Indian reservations. Gaming was divided into three classes. Class one gaming consisted of traditional Indian games. These were regulated by the tribes without non-Indian oversight. Class two gaming consisted mainly of bingo games. Initially these were to be regulated by a National Indian Gaming Commission also created by the Act, but after two years bingo was to be self-regulated by the tribes. Class three gaming included all other games (casino games, racing, and lotteries, for example) and would be regulated in accordance with compacts negotiated between the tribes and state governments. Indians could conduct games only if they were permitted by the state. The three-member National Indian Gaming Commission included two Indians and one non-Indian. In addition to providing general management of Indian gaming, the Commission was designed to outline gaming rules.

Charity Games Advertising Act of 1988
(Public Law 100-625, 7 November 1988)

The provisions of federal law prohibiting the use of the mail for advertising of gambling events and activities do not apply to charitable gaming.

Federal Reserve System Act, 1967 Amendments
(Public Law 90-203, 15 December 1967, Section 2)

Prohibited banks from dealing in lottery tickets, or advertising or announcing any gambling events.

Gambling Devices Act (Johnson Act)
(Public Law 906, 2 January 1951)

Gambling devices may not be transported across state lines, unless the machines are legal in the states involved. Gambling machines must be licensed and records of sales registered.

Federal Communications Act of 1934
(Public Act 416, 19 June 1934)

Advertisements regarding gambling were prohibited on radio or television broadcasts. However, amendments in 1975 (Public Act 94-526, passed 17 October 1976) made certain exceptions for state-sponsored lotteries.

Mail Frauds Act
(17 U.S. Stat. 302, 8 June 1872)

No letter or circular concerning illegal lotteries shall be carried in the mail. The word "illegal" was taken out of the act in 1876 (19 U.S. Stat. 90).

National Canadian Legislation

The Canadian Parliament's national criminal code has undergone tremendous change, moving from almost total prohibition to delegating responsibilities for gaming regulation to the provinces.

Criminal Code of Canada
(Section 189, 1892)

The code prohibited the operation of a gambling house, gambling in public places, and the conduct of lotteries. Cheating was also prohibited in any private game.

Criminal Code of Canada
(Section 190, 1969)

The provincial governments were given the authority to conduct lottery schemes and to authorize charitable organizations to conduct such schemes for fund-raising purposes. Government-run lotteries began as did many bingo operations. The notion of a scheme soon expanded to casino-type gaming. However, the code prohibited the use of dice in games as well as betting on single sports events. The code also prohibited organizations other than the provincial governments from utilizing machines for gambling.

Criminal Code of Canada
(Sections 189, 190, 1985)

Parliament placed the control of gambling activities under the jurisdiction of the provincial governments. The federal government yielded its own authority to run a national lottery in exchange for a collective contribution from provincial lottery revenues of $100 million to the support of the Calgary Winter Olympic Games. The new law continued a ban on nonprovincial machine gaming (gaming with dice) and wagering on single sports events.

Selected State and Provincial Legislation

British Columbia Lottery Act of 1974

British Columbia created a Lottery Branch (which was later placed in the attorney general's office) in order to conduct a provincial lottery and also to license charitable gaming events. In 1987 a British Columbia Gaming Commission was created to establish policy for gaming in the province.

Colorado Limited Gaming Act of 1991
(Colorado Rev. Stat. Ann. Sections 12-47.1-101 to 12-47.1-1401)

Subsequent to a vote of the people in November 1990, the Colorado legislature created the Colorado Limited Gaming Commission, comprised of five members and authorized to license casinos in the towns of Blackhawk, Central City, and Cripple Creek. Games of blackjack, poker, and machines are permitted with individual bets limited to $5. Tax rates for gross gaming proceeds are determined by the commission annually, but may not exceed 40 percent.

Illinois Riverboat Gambling Act
(1990 Ill. Laws 86-1029; Ill. Ann. Stat. ch. 120, Sections 2401-2423)

The act created the Illinois Gaming Board and authorized granting of licenses for up to ten casino riverboats in navigable waters of the state—excluding Lake Michigan and rivers in Cook County (Chicago). Casino revenues are taxed at a rate of 20 percent, with one-fourth of the amount going to local governments that permit the boats to take on passengers in their communities.

Iowa Riverboat Gaming Legislation
(1989 Iowa Act 67, 27 April 1989)

The Iowa State Racing and Gaming Commission is empowered to license casino boats to be docked in communities that approve them. Players may wager up to $5 per bet, and no more than $200 during an excursion cruise. Gaming revenues are taxed at rates up to 20 percent. Betting limits were removed in 1994.

Louisiana Casino Legislation for New Orleans
(La. Rev. Stat. Ann. 4.601 seq., 1992)

The legislature created the Louisiana Economic Development Gaming Corporation to license one land-based casino to be located at the site of the Rivergate Convention Center in downtown New Orleans. The legislation stated that a casino operation must lease the facilities from the city and also pay the state an annual tax of $100 million or 18.5 percent of gaming revenues—whichever is greater.

Louisiana Riverboat Casino Legislation
(La. Rev. Stat. Ann. Sections 4.501 seq., 1991)

The Louisiana legislature authorized unlimited casino gambling on certain rivers and waters of the state. The legislation designated the Riverboat Gaming Commission to grant licenses to as many as 15 boats, with casino revenues taxed at a rate of 18.5 percent.

Manitoba Lotteries Foundation Act (1982)

The Province of Manitoba created a gaming agency to centralize lottery operations and regulations of charity gaming. Subsequent regulations (28-84) gave the foundation the authority to conduct bingo and casino gaming on behalf of charities and Manitoba. The foundation became the sole operator of casinos soon afterward.

Mississippi Casino Gaming Act of 1991
(Miss. Code Ann. Sec. 75-76-7)

In 1991 the state of Mississippi created a three-member commission to license casino vessels for operation in certain designated waterways. The act allowed gaming activity to occur while the boats were permanently docked to the shore instead of only when they were taking cruises, as was the case in other riverboat gambling states. The act also permitted unlimited gaming and established a tax rate of up to 8 percent on gross gambling wins of the casinos.

Nevada Gaming Control Act
(Nevada Rev. Stat. Ann. Sections 463.010 seq. 1955 and
subsequent years, notably 1957, 1959, 1969, and 1983.)

The Nevada Gaming Control Act was first passed in 1931. As amended, the act currently states that the three-member Gaming

Control Board investigate applicants, make recommendations for licensing, and oversee gaming in state casinos. The five-member Nevada Gaming Commission is responsible for granting licenses and designing regulations for casino operations. Additionally, casinos pay a 6.25 percent tax on their gross gaming wins.

New Jersey Casino Control Act of 1977
(1977 N.J. Laws, 110; N.J. Stat. Ann. Sections 5-12-1 to 5-12-190)

Following a vote of the people in 1976, the New Jersey legislature enacted a law implementing the legalization of casinos for Atlantic City. The act created the Casino Control Commission to license casinos following recommendations from the Gaming Division within the state attorney general's office. The act maintains strict rules for casino operations and financing. Casino gaming revenues are taxed at a rate of 8 percent of gross gaming wins, plus additional fees for economic development projects for Atlantic City.

New York Off-Track Betting Law
(Laws of New York, Chapters 143, 144, 145, 22 April 1970)

New York established off-track pari-mutuel betting on horse races. Provisions allowed off-track parlors to be located both in New York City and State. Two government corporations were created to conduct the activity and to take out percentages of the wagers for tax purposes. Local governments throughout New York State were given the option of allowing parlors in their communities.

South Dakota Gaming Control Act
(S.D. Cod. Laws Ann. 42-7B-1 seq., 1988)

South Dakota voters authorized casino gaming for the town of Deadwood. The act allowed casinos to be licensed by the South Dakota Gaming Commission and deemed poker, blackjack, and machine gaming as permissible. Bets on single plays were limited to $5. Attempts to raise the maximum limits to $100 were later defeated by the voters. The act also requires casino revenues to be taxed at a rate of 8 percent.

Major Court Cases

Horner v. United States, 147 U.S. 449 (1893)

The Supreme Court upheld federal legislation ruling that the mails could not be used to transport lottery materials. The court defined the three elements of a lottery as (1) involving money or something of value (called consideration) being (2) offered in a game with a degree of risk, in hope of (3) securing something of greater value (prize).

Federal Communications Commission v. American Broadcasting Association, 347 U.S. 284 (1954)

The Supreme Court upheld the Federal Communications Commission's regulations prohibiting the broadcasting of information concerning lotteries.

Lewis v. United States, 348 U.S. 419 (1955)

The court ruled that a federal law providing for an occupational tax on wagering does not give parties the right to conduct gambling operations contrary to state and local regulations—including the regulations of the District of Columbia.

State v. Rosenthal, 93 Nev. 36, 559 P.2d. 830 (1977) Dismissed 434 U.S. 803 (1977)

The court found that there are no general constitutional rights to engage in the business of gambling. It is a privileged business subject to state control.

Seminole Indians v. Butterworth, 658 F. 2d 310 (5th Cir. 1981)

A precursor to the Cabazon Case. The court concluded that once a form of gambling is legalized in a state, the state loses the power to regulate such gaming on Indian reservation lands.

Posadas De Puerto Rico Associates v. Tourism Company of Puerto Rico, 478 U.S. 328 (1986)

The United States Supreme Court upheld the constitutionality of a Puerto Rico statute, which prohibited advertising of casino gambling.

The court reasoned that the casino industry was a special industry, and that the commonwealth had the power to protect its citizens by limiting their exposure to the industry.

Cabazon v. California, 480 U.S. 202 (1987)

The United States Supreme Court upheld the right of Indian tribes to conduct gaming on their reservations as long as the gaming was not in violation of the general policy and criminal law of the state. The gaming was not subject to the civil regulations of the state, as the state had only criminal jurisdiction on reservation lands. The ruling was an important factor in Congress's decision to pass the Indian Gaming Regulatory Act of 1988, which outlined the regulation of gambling activities on Indian reservations.

GNOC Corp. v. Shmuel Aboud, United States District Court, New Jersey; 715 Fed. Supp. 644 (1989)

The Golden Nugget Casino of Atlantic City brought an action against Mr. Aboud to recover debts he incurred while a player at the casino. Aboud entered a counterclaim asserting that the casino had intentionally served him alcoholic beverages to intoxicate him so that he would engage in reckless gambling activities. The court stated that it was the casino's duty to refrain from accepting bets from intoxicated players, and that the casino could be held liable if they did accepts such bets. The court, however, held for the casino due to the fact that the player was unable to prove his claim. This was the first case indicating that a casino may be liable for encouraging intoxicated people to gamble.

Erickson v. Desert Palace, United States Court of Appeals for the Ninth Circuit, 21 August 1991. Cert. Denied United States Supreme Court.

On 5 August 1987, Kirk Erickson, a tourist from Arkansas, played a slot machine at Caesars Palace in Las Vegas, Nevada. Erickson inserted three one-dollar tokens into a slot machine, pulled the handle, and lined up certain winning symbols. According to the casino's display, he had won $1,061,812. However, Caesars Palace refused to pay Erickson, a 19-year-old, because he was underage. (In Nevada a person must be 21 years old to gamble in a casino.) The court held that the plaintiff (Erickson) must seek relief through administrative law processes in the state of Nevada. The Nevada Gaming Control Board denied Erickson's claim because the debt in question was illegal and hence, unenforceable through legal action. Consequently, Erickson received no payment from Caesars Palace.

Points of View

To scrimp and save to lay by a few pounds to see these eroded by inflation, wiped out and exposed in their foolish inadequacy in a sudden family emergency or, worst of all, to leave your few accumulated possessions to be fought over when you die—no other single cause, by all accounts, exerts comparable power as a detonator of family unity—is poor sense. To use this money in the hope of a big strike—who knows, you might even win enough to put down a deposit on a house—is surely superior rationality.

Otto Newman, *Gambling: Hazard and Reward* (1972, 228).

You must realize that a working-class chap is an underdog and feels like one. He is not satisfied with present conditions, so he often escapes into a world of dreams. This world he finds in religion, socialism, or gambling. Socialism is a dream for himself personally. He can't hope to save enough to get out of his dreary existence. He can't work himself up, that is open only to a few of the best men. The only way out of the mines, or cotton mills, or foundry work . . . is to win in a big way. Only in that way can he gain his real freedom.

Peter Fuller, *The Psychology of Gambling* (1974, 35).

Legalized casino gambling has been approved by the citizens of New Jersey as a unique tool of urban redevelopment for Atlantic City . . . to attract new investment capital to New Jersey in general and Atlantic City in particular.

New Jersey Casino Control Act, 1977.

Some people say casino gambling is the best way to get new jobs. New industries and casino gambling simply do not go together. In the last few years, we have built up momentum in bringing new jobs to Florida, because we have fine weather, no personal income tax, and stable government. Casinos will severely damage these efforts to bring challenging, high-paying jobs to our people throughout Florida. Casinos are a bad risk. Who needs casino gambling? We don't.

Florida Governor Reubin Askew, 1978 anticasino commercial.

You're going to find Mormons here who say, "Oh, I just hate gaming." Well, that's silly. You like the roads you drive on? Gaming paid for them. You like the schools your kids go to? Gaming paid for them. You like the parks? Gaming paid for them. Face it: If you live in Nevada, you have to accept gaming. It pays the bills.

The late Joe Burt, a Mormon and general manager of Aladdin Hotel Casino in Las Vegas. *Las Vegas Review Journal* (13 July 1992, 4B).

There's been a transformation in the way the [Mormon] Church views southern Nevada. The reason gaming and the Church have gotten along so well here is we've grown up together. . . . The business of gaming has attained legitimacy. The Mob is gone. We now have major publicly traded corporations in the business. The whole management fiber of gaming has changed.

Richard Bunker, a Mormon and executive director of the Nevada Resorts Association. *Las Vegas Review Journal* (13 July 1992, 4B).

Regulation is important to assure public confidence in the integrity of the games and to increase public acceptance by removing any perception that criminals have ownership interest in the casinos. Governments should also be aware that regulation can inadvertently stifle the growth of an industry. If the goal of a jurisdiction is to use casino gaming to stimulate tourism and raise revenue, the best regulatory system will achieve its regulatory goals at the least cost to the regulated and with the least interference with the operators' business judgment. This is important in a world economy with increased competition.

Casino operators must be responsible in exercising their business judgment. Casino gaming should be a recreational activity primarily for those on a vacation, not something that government needs or wants to encourage as a tenet of daily life for its residents. If casinos, or governments, in their quest to raise gaming revenues seek not the recreational dollar but their own residents' earnings, the public may soon sour on the experiment.

Grant Sawyer, governor of Nevada, 1959–1967. "Foreword" to *International Casino Law* (2d ed., 1993).

The casinos now allow Native Americans to be involved in large-scale economy and work in a capitalistic area. You have enough dollars to provide more social services to your people. If you are going to work in a capitalist world, then you have to adapt to the policies of the capitalist world. Not all of them, but most of them.

Leonard Prescott, chairman of the board, Mystic Lake and Little Six Casinos, Shakopee-Mdewakanton Sioux Community, Minnesota. *Indian Gaming* (January 1993,11).

Among the pleasures of gambling, certainly the greatest is winning. Anyone who has ever had a two-dollar bet pay off or the contents of the pot shoved his way knows that special exaltation that comes from a combination of pride in skill and joy at the sense of accomplishment. To beat the system with your own system—that is a fulfilling experience. Of course, there is nothing wrong with winning if you don't have a system. Pure luck, when it descends on you of all people, can give you a feeling of gratified self-importance comparable to few other delights.

David Newman, *Esquire's Book of Gambling* (1962, 13).

Losing well is important if (a) you want to be invited back, or (b) you want to be known as a good loser. However, if you lose well many times over a period of a year, you might consider the possibility that you are not only a good loser but a loser. Your move then is to learn what you're doing wrong, or curse the fates and take up painting. There are, unfortunately, many gamblers who can't quit that easily. For them, the perils are many and the consequences are devastating. In recent years psychologists have attempted to learn the motivations behind the overpowering need to risk everything on a roll of the dice or a spin of the wheel. When gambling assumes its proper place in the spectrum of behavior, it functions as amusement and furnishes a bit of excitement. But for those who are, in the truest sense, addicted, the enticements become daily and deadly necessities. Such is the lot of the compulsive, the habitual gambler.

David Newman, *Esquire's Book of Gambling* (1962, 27).

Lottery proponents argue many wagered dollars stimulate local economies through expenditures on advertising and retail sales commissions. However, very few people living in the ghettos and barrios own television networks or newspaper chains. Likewise, a majority of lottery ticket outlets in the country are owned by corporations. Even independently owned outlets are seldom, if ever, owned by anyone in the low-income category. Lottery dollars follow a one-way street out of the poorest neighborhoods, and few, if any, of these dollars ever find their way back into the areas from whence they came.

Alan Karcher (former New Jersey state senator), *Lotteries* (1989, 96–97).

It is essential to recognize that the lotteries, in the absence of a destructive scandal, are here to stay. It is just as important to acknowledge that lotteries have had some undeniable, though limited, benefits. Lottery revenues have eased some budget pressures, and to a limited degree, allowed for the real expansion of some worthwhile programs. But these benefits have only been realized at a cost—a cost that is becoming increasingly heavier when measured in terms of existing abuses, potential exploitation that must come with a system driven by the imperative for increased revenue, and the risk of budgetary disorder inherent in the advance appropriation of speculative income.

Alan Karcher (former New Jersey state senator), *Lotteries* (1989, 113).

It is fundamentally immoral to encourage the belief by the people as a whole in gambling as a source of family income. It would be immoral for government to make available to all of its people a statewide gambling apparatus with the implied assumption that the gains of chance were a fair substitute for or supplement to the honorable business of producing the goods and services by which the people of the nation live. It would be an indecent thing for government to finance itself so largely out of the weaknesses of the people which it had deliberately encouraged that a large share of its revenue would come from gambling. I recognize that the state and some municipalities now receive a comparatively small revenue from pari-mutuel betting at race tracks. I have always had personal doubts about the wisdom or the morality of this system but it is confined to those who are actually able to be present at the track and therefore is not a lure dangled before all people in all walks of life and near every home.

Thomas E. Dewey (former New York governor), special address to the New York State Legislature (16 January 1950).

Ultimately, pathological gambling results in crime. Studies . . . uncovered a wide variety of illegal behaviors among the compulsive gamblers interviewed. . . . Compulsive gamblers were involved in check forgery, embezzlement and employee theft, larceny, armed robbery, bookmaking, hustling, running con games, and fencing stolen goods. I . . . also found gamblers engaged in systematic loan fraud, tax evasion, burglary, pimping, prostitution, illicit drug sales, and hustling at pool, golf, bowling, cards and dice. . . . Compulsive gamblers are engaged in a spiral of options and involvement wherein legal avenues for funding are utilized until they are closed off. As involvement in gambling intensifies, options for legal funding are closed. Depending on personal value systems, legitimate and illegitimate opportunities, perceptions of risk, the existence of threats (for example, by loan sharks), and chance, many compulsive gamblers became involved in more and more serious illegal activity. For some of them, the amount of money runs into millions of dollars.

Henry Lesieur, "Pathological Gambling in Canada," in
Gambling in Canada: Golden Goose or Trojan Horse? (1989, 230).

Historically gambling has been considered a vice and even in many modern societies where legal gambling exists, it still remains morally tainted. Part of the reason for this censure concerns the risk that gambling necessarily involves. In one sense, gambling is nothing more than risk-taking in the hope of realizing some reward. The question is, if gambling is to be considered immoral or unethical because it involves a certain degree of risk, why are other activities involving risk not likewise considered unethical? We are constantly exposed to choices involving different degrees and types of risk. The level of risk which is comfortable for one person may be deemed totally foolhardy by others. Risk merely means that a decision is made to engage in an activity with an uncertain outcome. In the case of gambling the uncertainty relates to the receipt of a monetary reward, and it is this which makes it different from other forms of entertainment.

Charles Singer, "The Ethics of Gambling," in *Gambling in Canada: Golden Goose or Trojan Horse?* (1989, 277–278).

The most powerful argument put forward by the critics of large-scale gambling—particularly by the political left and welfare groups—is the fear that social and moral structures will be undermined by . . . forms of commercial gambling. Concern was expressed . . . that Canada's traditional emphasis on charity gambling will be brutalized or swallowed up by competitive commercialism. They warn that the generous social programs built up over the years from gambling revenues could be abandoned by future governments as Canadian gambling becomes private and corporate.

Jan McMillen, "The Future," in *Gambling in Canada: Golden Goose or Trojan Horse?* (1989, 397).

Fifty-five million in Florida. Sixty-two million in California. Sixty-nine million in Illinois. And now 115 million dollars in Pennsylvania. Wonderful for the states, and even more wonderful for the few lucky winners, but in the long run these astronomical jackpots may not be good for the lottery industry. For despite widespread public acceptance of lotteries, there are still those who hold the get-rich-quick lure of the lottery is a repudiation of the cherished American work ethic. Those sentiments gain currency whenever lotto jackpots reach stratospheric levels. And they're encouraged by inevitable media accounts of would-be multimillionaires mortgaging their homes to buy tickets. Perhaps the time has come for the lottery industry to reconsider the concept of capping prizes at some reasonable level—say $50 million—before the naysayers begin to make sense.

Paul Dworin, editor of *Gaming and Wagering Business* (15 May 1989, 5.)

Las Vegas has done such a fantastic job in positioning itself as the gaming capital of the world that any other community that hoped to compete with Las Vegas would have to come to the conclusion that it wants to be number one. But if they were to do that, it would take years. It took Las Vegas 15 years from the time it created this vision 'til now, when they have 22 million visitors and they are the third-highest tourism destination market in the U.S.

John Boushy, vice president of Harrah's Casino Hotels, quoted in *Gaming and Wagering Business* (May 15–June 15, 1993, 10.)

Indian peoples have known for many years sovereignty is a double-edged sword. On one hand, it gives Native Americans advantages, at least in the world of gaming, that non-Indians don't enjoy. In states where commercial, non-Indian casinos are illegal, Indian tribes often can use sovereignty as a tool to launch their own casinos. And the tax burden for Indian-run casinos is far less than a commercial business would have to bear. That's the positive side of sovereignty. It is the side of the issue that has given reservation economies an enormous boost and allowed Indian tribes to escape the grinding cycle of poverty and despair. But now millions of dollars are flowing through Indian reservation casinos every day. People who have for years known nothing but deprivation are suddenly having unimaginably huge amounts of money thrown at them, sometimes by unscrupulous individuals. Tribal leaders are being lavished with attentions they're not all used to. . . . Entertaining potential clients and offering them little gifts is certainly within the bounds of standard business practices. But the danger occurs if the tribal leadership becomes too cozy with a management company that doesn't have the tribe's best interest in mind. . . . So tribal

members who suspect their elected leadership has been co-opted
by a corrupt management company have almost no recourse. State
and federal government bodies, when dealing with tribes, are really
dealing with tribal councils, whether or not those councils are acting
in the best interests of the tribe. That is not to say organized crime
infiltration of Indian casinos is commonplace or that every tribal
government is corrupt. But, just as with any government official,
it does exist.

Matt Connor, *Gaming and Wagering Business* (October 15–November 14, 1993,
1, 55).

That position is strongly disputed by Rick Hill, the newly elected
chairman of the National Indian Gaming Association. Referring
to a report last year from the Department of Justice that said
the "perception in the media and elsewhere that Indian gaming
operations are rife with serious criminality does not stand up
under close examination," Hill flatly denied . . . charges of
organized crime infiltration of reservation casinos. "There is no
organized crime, reorganized crime, or disorganized crime on
Indian reservations," Hill said, . . . "what critics of Indian gaming
are really afraid of is organized Indians."

Matt Connor, *Gaming and Wagering Business* (July 15–August 14, 1993, 44–45).

Illegal sports betting in the United States is a huge business. Last
year alone, bettors wagered billions of dollars with illegal book-
makers. Every major newspaper prints wagering information.
Customers spend millions of dollars on services that claim to
have an advantage in picking winners based on the current line.
Some even claim that illegal betting is the reason that professional
sports have gained the popularity that they enjoy. The problem with
keeping sports betting illegal is that the illegality itself does not solve
the problem. Persons do not cease to bet on sports simply because it
is illegal. This is because in most societies, the enforcement of crimes
usually falls into two categories: zero tolerance or decriminalized. The
former is reserved for crimes that are strictly and severely punished,
with the goal of total eradication. The latter are tolerated crimes that
occur almost freely, and aren't severely punished when pursued.
Sports wagering is the latter. The problem with decriminalized crimes
is that, by definition, criminals run the operation. Money derived from
these operations can be funnelled into other criminal activities. Police
are more likely to accept graft to protect the illegal operators. Regular
citizens lose respect for the criminal justice system. And just as

important, no regulatory system insures the honesty of the operations. Because of the involvement of the criminal element in the wagering activities, sports are more apt, not less likely, to be tainted with scandal.

Anthony Cabot, *Casino Journal* (December 1993,12).

When you don't have control over your betting habit, it's an illness, like alcoholism or nicotine dependency. The main symptom is likely to be depression. If you bet money that you can't afford to lose, and then you lose, you are going to feel down. How do you come up with the money when you don't have it? Borrow? Hell, just double your previous bet! That way you still end up winning, right? Wrong! You never know how long your bad luck will last. If it lasts too long, and you can't afford to play, you might find yourself in a heap of trouble. It's not something that you ever want to experience.

Vincent Kray, a Toronto gambler, in *You Bet: Canada's Gaming Report* (February 1994, 19).

The Cabazon and Morongo Reservations contain no natural resources which can be exploited. The tribal games at present provide the sole source of revenues for the operation of the tribal governments and the provision of tribal services. They are also the major sources of employment on the reservations. Self-determination and economic development are not within reach if the tribes cannot raise revenues and provide employment for their members.

Justice Byron White, *Cabazon v. California,* 480 U.S. 202 (1987).

Sec. 2. The Congress finds that. . . . Indians have the exclusive right to regulate gaming activity on Indian lands if the gaming activity is not specifically prohibited by federal law and is conducted within a State which does not, as a matter of criminal law and public policy, prohibit such gaming activity. . . .

Sec. 3. The purpose of this Act is—(1) to provide a statutory basis for the operation of gaming by Indian tribes as a means of promoting tribal economic development, self-sufficiency, and strong tribal governments; (2) to provide a statutory basis for the regulation of gaming by an Indian tribe adequate to shield it from organized crime and other corrupting influences, to ensure that the Indian tribe is the primary beneficiary of the gaming operation, and to assure that gaming is conducted fairly and honestly by both the operator and players. . . .

From the Indian Gaming Regulatory Act, Public Law 100-497 (17 October 1988).

Gambling is the only business, legal or illegal, where the product being sold is cash, with no paper record. Organized crime is always attracted to cash businesses, but so is unorganized crime. The high-tech security systems found in every large casino are there to watch for cheating and stealing by employees more than by players. Every government that has legalized gambling has soon realized that it has had to institute tough controls, and most have found that the criminals can be a lot smarter than the regulators.

I. Nelson Rose, professor of law at Whittier College of Law, in *Indian Gaming and the Law* (1990, 6–7).

It's no secret that I was opposed to expanding gaming on Indian Lands. I think that it is still a poor tool for economic development in Indian Country and the social ills that it is likely to bring with it may completely overshadow and economic benefits. In Nevada, we understand the social costs associated with large scale commercial gaming, and we've learned over the more than fifty years of its legal existence to deal with it and compensate for it.

U.S. Senator Harry Reid (Nevada), in *Indian Gaming and the Law* (1990, 15).

The gradual decline in police responsibility for gambling enforce-ment has many roots. The entry of state governments into various forms of gambling certainly was important. So was the federal campaign against large-scale gambling organizations. I would also speculate that increased popular understanding of the inevitable failure of gambling enforcement and a concern that police devote their limited resources to other, more pressing activities may have been the most significant factors. . . . [G]ambling is no longer a major problem for local police. Few resources are devoted to it, except for the occasional large-scale raid, it is given little attention. Narcotics enforcement has apparently taken its place as the responsibility that poses the greatest threat to police autonomy.

Peter Reuter, "Police Regulation of Illegal Gambling," in *The Annals of the American Academy of Political and Social Sciences* (July 1984, 47).

The prostitute, the pimp, the peddler of dope, the operator of the gambling hall, the vendor of obscene pictures, the bootlegger, the abortionist, all are productive, all produce goods or services which people desire and for which they are willing to pay. It happens that society has put these goods and services under the ban, but people go on producing them and people go on consuming them, and an act of the legislature does not make them any less a part of the economic system.

Edward Hawkins and Willard W. Waller, *Critical Notes on the Cost of Crime* (1936, 684–685).

Leonard Tose, the former owner of the Philadelphia Eagles National Football League team, admitted on the witness stand in federal court in Camden yesterday that the first time he signed a marker for $30,000 at the Sands Casino in Atlantic City he was too drunk to remember it. Tose, 77, is suing to recover some of the $14 million he admits losing there. Tose claims casino employees encouraged him to drink and then took advantage of him while he was intoxicated. His suit lists 42 dates between 16 June 1981 and 31 December 1982, when he lost $9,740,000 at the Sands, and 30 dates between 10 May 1985 and 2 April 1986 when he lost an additional $4,930,000.

Joseph D. McCaffrey, in *The Star Ledger* (18 February 1993).

Frank Twiggs, a certified compulsive gambling counselor and a member of the Council on Compulsive Gambling in New Jersey, said Monday that statistics indicate underage gambling is a serious problem. In 1991, the casinos reported that nearly 200,000 people under age 21 were turned away at the doors, while 20,000 others were asked to leave the floor, Twiggs said. "Everybody acknowledges that it's a problem," he said. "The number of kids who are gambling—any form of gambling—is reaching 100%."

Trudy Walz, in *The Record* (North Jersey) (31 August 1993).

Figures and Tables

Figure 4.1 is a map portraying casino gaming in the United States. Commercial casino gambling has spread to 10 states, with river-boat casino gambling offered in 6 states and land-based casinos present in 5 states; there is 1 state with charity casino games offered on a daily basis in permanent locations, and Indian reservation casino gaming is now present in 16 states. (See page 112.)

FIGURE 4.1
Casino Gaming in the United States

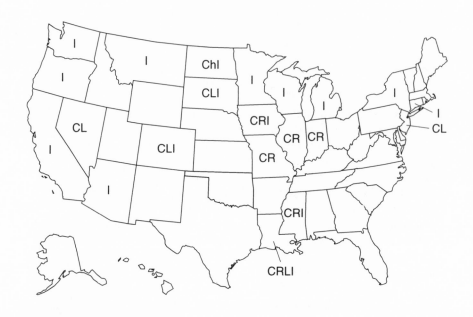

C	Commercial
G	Government
Ch	Charity-Permanent
R	Riverboats
L	Landbased
I	Indian

Casino gaming has now spread from Quebec westward across the remainder of the Canadian provinces. While most of their gaming is charity based, government-owned casinos have been authorized for Manitoba, Ontario, and Quebec. (See Figure 4.2, page 113.)

The dates of casino and lottery legalizations demonstrate that policy makers of states and provinces often have a tendency to adopt the same kind of gaming activity that has been legalized in bordering states. Gambling legalization can protect states by offering games that will keep their residents from gambling in other

FIGURE 4.2
Casino Gaming in Canada

C   Commercial
G   Government
Ch Charity-Permanent
R   Riverboats
L   Landbased
I   Indian

states. However, states are also inclined to follow policies of nearby states due to frequent communication and an increased familiarity with gambling. (See Figure 4.3, page 114; and Figure 4.4, page 115.)

Thirty-seven states and the District of Columbia have authorized government-run lotteries. In addition, seven of these states have permitted the placement of video gaming machines in their territories. These machines are typically called "video lottery terminals" and are almost identical to video slot machines found in commercial casinos, except that prize money is awarded with tickets rather than with actual coin drops. The gaming machines offer

FIGURE 4.3
Dates of Commercial Casino Legalizations

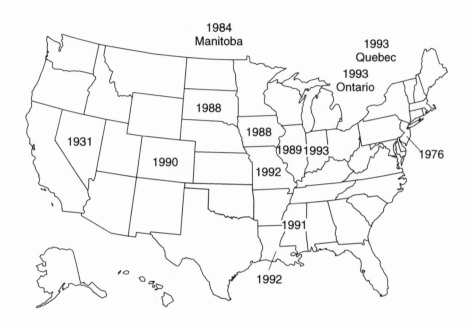

play at simulated games of poker, blackjack, and keno. (See Figure 4.5, page 116.)

Every province of Canada has a government run lottery. Three western provinces—Manitoba, Saskatchewan, and Alberta—and four eastern provinces—New Brunswick, Nova Scotia, Prince Edward's Island, and Newfoundland—offer multiprovince lotteries. Individually, these same seven provinces allow video lottery machines similar to those offered in the seven states below the border. (See Figure 4.4, page 115; and Figure 4.6, page 117.)

The overwhelming majority of states offer forms of parimutuel betting: prizes are awarded from a common pool made up of the players' money. While the betting organization (the track) does not participate in the gambling, it draws a fee from the pool for administering the wagering among the players. The most popular form of pari-mutuel betting is on horse races, followed by dog

FIGURE 4.4
Dates of Lottery Beginnings

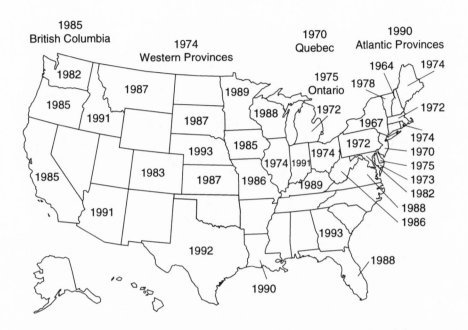

races. Four states permit such betting on jai alai matches. Several states have legalized off-track betting and intertrack betting (a player at one track bets on races at other tracks). (See Figure 4.7, page 118.) Every province in Canada has horse-race betting. Six of the ten provinces have intertrack betting. (See Figure 4.8, page 119.)

Gross gaming revenues have increased three-fold in the period between 1982 to 1992. The revenues from lotteries have grown the fastest, while casino growth has also been dramatic. On the other hand, pari-mutuel wagering has remained for the most part static. Only with the advent of off-track and intertrack wagering has this sector grown at all. (See Figure 4.9, page 120.)

FIGURE 4.5
Lotteries in the United States

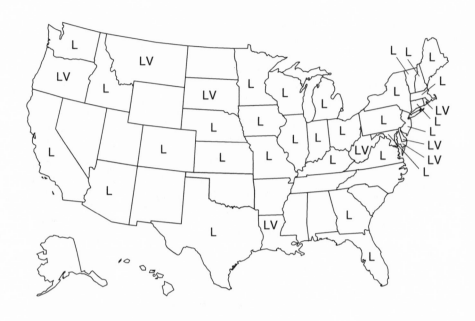

L	Government Run Lottery
V	Video Lottery Terminals

Today lotteries lead the gaming industry in terms of revenues, followed by casinos and pari-mutuels. In future years dramatic increases in Indian reservation revenues are expected, and many more new casino facilities are being opened by American Indians. (See Figure 4.10, page 121.)

The road to a compulsive gambling career is a road of selfish false dreams. It is often a very quick journey. Recovery is a slow path toward reality and concern for others. A leading group that supports those in recovery has depicted the many stages on the path toward destruction and the path back to responsibility. (See Figure 4.11, page 122.)

Lottery revenues bring billions to state governments. Tables 4.1 and 4.2 show the source of the revenues and their disposition with United States and Canadian lotteries. The average per capita ticket sales are just over $100 in the United States (in lottery

FIGURE 4.6
Lotteries in Canada

L Government Run Lottery
V Video Lottery Terminals

jurisdictions) and $167 in Canada. Prizes returned to players rep-
resent about one-half of the sales, while administrative expenses
equalled about 11 percent in the United States and 17 percent in
Canada. Governments retain about three-eights of the amounts
wagered. (See Table 4.1, page 123; and 4.2, page 124.)

Tables 4.3, 4.4, and 4.5 illustrate that voters view various
kinds of gambling activity differently. Although there has been a
rush toward casino legalizations in recent years, the voters exhibit
much more reluctance to legalize casinos than other forms of
gambling. Lotteries are quite popular and usually pass with overwhelming votes when placed on the ballot. Election votes on pari-
mutuel legalization have mixed results, while majorities of the
public are most often negative on casino legalization questions.
The spread of casino legalization has come, for the most part,
from action in state and provincial legislative assemblies. (See
Tables 4.3, 4.4, and 4.5, pages 125–127.)

FIGURE 4.7
Pari-Mutuel Wagering in the United States

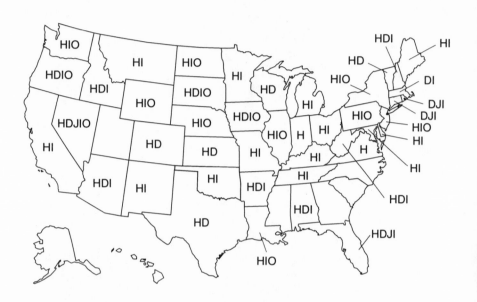

H	Horse Racing
D	Dog Racing
J	Jai Alai
O	Offtrack
I	Intertrack

FIGURE 4.8
Pari-Mutuel Wagering in Canada

H   Horse Racing
D   Dog Racing
J   Jai Alai
O   Offtrack
I   Intertrack

FIGURE 4.9
Gross Gaming Wins by Category, 1982–1992

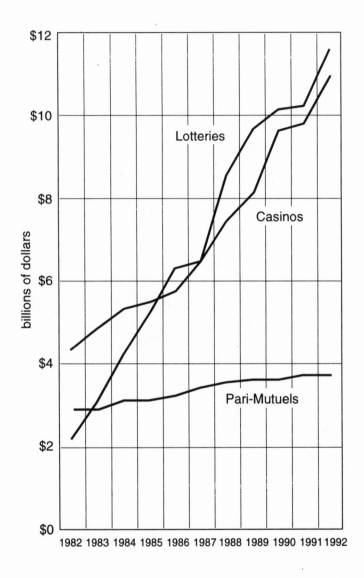

FIGURE 4.10
Gross Revenue from Legal Gambling, 1992

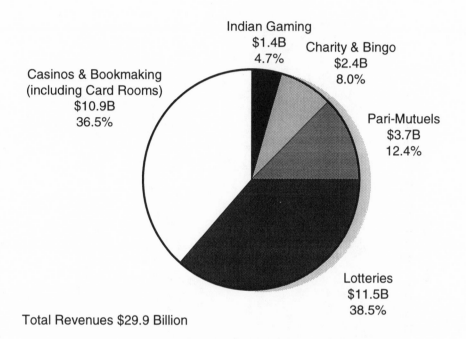

Indian Gaming
$1.4B
4.7%

Charity & Bingo
$2.4B
8.0%

Casinos & Bookmaking
(including Card Rooms)
$10.9B
36.5%

Pari-Mutuels
$3.7B
12.4%

Lotteries
$11.5B
38.5%

Total Revenues $29.9 Billion

Source: Gaming & Wagering Business (August 15-September 14, 1993)

FIGURE 4.11
A Chart of Compulsive Gambling and Recovery

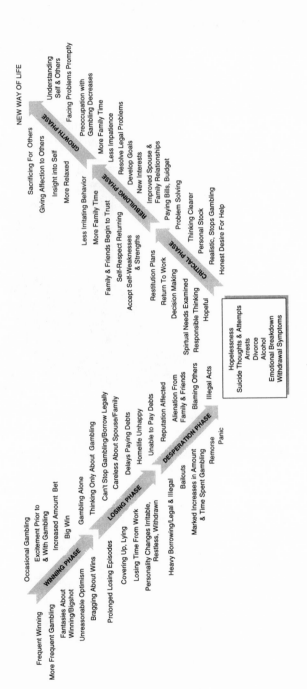

Source: Reprinted, courtesy of Arnie & Sheila Wexler Associates.

TABLE 4.1

U.S. Lottery Performance, FY 1992 (in millions of dollars)

State Lottery	Ticket Sales	P.C. Sales	Prizes	Expenses	Net Income
Arizona	249.3	$65	119.3	38.4	91.6
California	1,358.7	$44	669.2	224.6	464.9
Colorado	239.2	$69	125.0	37.3	76.9
Connecticut	543.8	$166	288.6	50.7	204.5
District of Columbia	147.0	$213	79.4	19.1	48.5
Delaware	78.1	$133	41.5	8.9	27.7
Florida	2,174.6	$161	1,091.4	221.1	862.1
Idaho	51.7	$48	28.1	11.0	12.6
Illinois	1,579.6	$136	815.1	152.3	612.2
Indiana	390.1	$69	216.0	57.9	116.2
Iowa	166.3	$59	92.9	27.4	46.0
Kansas	77.2	$31	37.3	16.1	23.8
Kentucky	426.5	$114	263.3	59.8	103.4
Louisiana	380.2	$89	192.0	48.6	139.6
Maine	114.1	$92	61.4	17.2	35.5
Maryland	812.3	$165	394.3	75.1	342.9
Massachusetts	1,860.9	$310	1,172.4	168.5	520.0
Michigan	1,218.5	$129	612.4	128.8	477.3
Minnesota	297.6	$66	172.6	50.6	74.4
Missouri	220.4	$42	115.3	38.0	67.1
Montana	27.9	$34	13.6	8.7	5.6
New Hampshire	111.2	$100	53.6	20.9	36.7
New Jersey	1,360.3	$175	680.0	106.1	574.2
New York	2,063.1	$114	968.7	227.7	866.7
Ohio	1,685.4	$153	888.2	150.1	647.1
Oregon	268.0	$90	140.8	54.3	72.9
Pennsylvania	1,408.9	$117	623.0	128.1	657.8
Rhode Island	64.6	$64	31.4	9.6	23.6
S. Dakota	60.7	$85	12.3	4.5	43.9
Texas	591.0	$33	269.0	119.0	203.0
Vermont	51.4	$90	27.8	6.7	16.9
Virginia	846.6	$133	454.3	101.5	290.8
Washington	302.2	$59	151.0	42.6	108.6
West Virginia	90.3	$50	46.5	14.5	29.3
Wisconsin	449.1	$90	258.7	39.8	150.6
Total	$21,767.1	$103	$11,206.4	$2,486.9	$8,073.8
	(100%)		(51.5%)	(11.4%)	(37.1%)

TABLE 4.2
Canadian Lottery Performance, FY 1992
(in hundreds of millions of dollars)

Lottery	Ticket Sales	P.C. Sales	Prizes	Expenses	Net Income
Atlantic	393.8	$171	158.8	110.8	124.2
B.C.	676.6	$221	337.8	114.0	224.8
Loto-Quebec	1,316.0	$197	629.5	202.0	484.5
Ontario	1,406.3	$147	674.2	234.4	497.7
W. Canada	580.5	$126	264.2	86.5	229.8
Total	$4,369.1	$167	$2,064.4	$747.7	$1,561.0
	(100%)		(47.2%)	(17.1%)	(35.7%)

TABLE 4.3
Selected Popular Referenda Votes (Lotteries)

Year	State	Percentage
1992	Nebraska	
	Georgia	
1991	Texas	65%
1990	Louisiana	69%
1988	Missouri	58%
	Indiana	62%
	Minnesota	59%
	Kentucky	61%
	Idaho	52%
1987	Virginia	57%
1986	Wisconsin	
	Florida	64%
	Montana	69%
	South Dakota	60%
	North Dakota	44% (Defeated)
1984	Missouri	68%
	California	58%
	Oregon	66%
	West Virginia	66%
1973	Rhode Island	76%
	Ohio	64%
	Maine	72%
1972	Maryland	77%
	Michigan	73%
	Iowa	67%
	Washington	62%
1966	New Jersey	81%

TABLE 4.4
Selected Popular Referenda Votes (Horseracing)

Year	State	Percentage
1988	Tennessee (local) Virginia Nebraska	49% (Defeated) 56% 62%
1987	Texas	56%
1986	Kansas	58%
1984	Missouri	60%
1982	Minnesota Oklahoma	58% 58%
1978	Virginia	48% (Defeated)
1974	Oklahoma	46% (Defeated)
1971	Missouri	46% (Defeated)
1968	Indiana	47% (Defeated)
1963	New York (OTB)	76%
1956	Arkansas	53%

TABLE 4.5
Selected Popular Referenda Votes (Casinos)

Year	State	Percentage
1994	Missouri	49% (Defeated)
1992	Missouri	58%
1990	Colorado Ohio Alaska North Dakota	56% 42% (Defeated) 40% (Defeated) 35% (Defeated)
1988	South Dakota	64%
1986	Florida	32% (Defeated)
1984	Colorado Arkansas	33% (Defeated) 29% (Defeated)
1978	Florida	27% (Defeated)
1976	New Jersey	56%
1974	New Jersey	40% (Defeated)
1964	Arkansas	39% (Defeated)

5

Directory of Organizations

Private Organizations

American Quarter Horse Association
2736 West Tenth
Amarillo, TX 79168
(806) 376-4811

This association maintains the registry for all racing quarter horses and publishes rules for quarter horse racing.

PUBLICATIONS: Rules for quarter horse racing.

Association of Racing Commissioners International, Inc.
Kentucky Horse Park
4067 Iron Works Pike
Lexington, KY 40511
(606) 278-5460

An association of government regulatory bodies. Its essential purpose is to exchange regulatory information and guarantee the security of the racing industry.

PUBLICATIONS: A weekly newsletter and annual compilation of statistics on race track activity in North America.

Canadian Foundation on Compulsive Gambling
505 Consumers Road, #605
Willowdale, Ontario
Canada M2J 4V8
(416) 499-9800

The Foundation supports the study of problem gambling and lobbies governments for funding of treatment programs.

Canadian Trotting Association
2150 Meadowdale Boulevard
Mississauga, Ontario
Canada L5N 6R6
(416) 858-3060

An association founded in 1939 to record and distribute information on harness racing in Canada. Members include track and horse owners, drivers, and trainers.

PUBLICATIONS: The monthly magazine *Trot* and a registry for standard bred horses in Canada.

Gamblers Anonymous
California Organization
P.O. Box 17173
Los Angeles, CA 90017
(213) 386-8789

Founded in 1957, Gamblers Anonymous has over 900 chapters worldwide. It is a self-help operation for problem gamblers and is patterned after Alcoholics Anonymous. Related chapters serve members of problem gamblers' families.

The Gambler's Book Club
630 South 11th Street
Las Vegas, NV 89101
(702) 382-7555

The Gambler's Book Club carries the world's largest supply of gaming books and related materials for sale.

PUBLICATIONS: A newsletter and catalogs listing the club's stock of books.

Harness Tracks of America, Inc.
35 Airport Road
Morristown, NJ 07960
(201) 285-9090

An association of track owners concerned with various aspects of harness racing, including marketing, security, and government relations.

PUBLICATIONS: A weekly newsletter.

The Institute for the Study of Gambling and Commercial Gaming
University of Nevada
Reno, NV 89557
(702) 784-1477

The institute conducts seminars for the gaming industry and sponsors international gaming conferences, which bring together scholars and industry leaders from around the world.

PUBLICATIONS: The proceedings from the conferences and a newsletter. The institute is also copublisher of the *Journal of Gambling Studies*.

International Association of Gaming Attorneys
P.O. Box 7438
Las Vegas, NV 89125
(702) 384-3840

The association conducts seminars and annual conventions for attorneys from around the world.

PUBLICATIONS: Treatises on gaming topics and information related to the current legal status of gaming in all jurisdictions.

International Association of State Lotteries
500 Sherbrooke Street, West, Suite 2000
Montreal, Quebec
Canada H3A 3G6
(514) 282-8000

Founded in 1958, the association fosters the exchange of ideas related to the technical aspects of lottery organization and operation.

PUBLICATIONS: A directory and industry review.

The Jockey Club
380 Madison Avenue
New York, NY 10017
(212) 599-1919

One of the original organizations created to monitor the integrity of racing in America. Founded in 1894, it serves a crucial function of maintaining a registry of thoroughbred race horses. The rules of the Jockey Club are a nationwide model for racing rules. The organization is patterned after the Jockey Club of the United Kingdom.

PUBLICATIONS: Registry of thoroughbred horses.

National Council on Compulsive Gambling
444 W. 56th Street
New York, NY 10019
(212) 763-3833

The council encourages public support for treatment programs for problem gamblers and holds regular educational conferences.

PUBLICATIONS: Copublishes the leading academic journal on gambling issues, the *Journal of Gambling Studies*.

National Greyhound Association
Box 543
Abilene, KS 67410
(913) 263-4660

The association maintains a registry of racing dogs and promotes the industry by lobbying and sponsoring seminars.

PUBLICATIONS: The monthly *Greyhound Review*.

National Indian Gaming Association
Delaware Tribe of Western Oklahoma
Box 806
Anadarko, OK 73005
(405) 247-2448

An association comprised of tribes and associated members engaged in gaming enterprises on reservations. The association promotes integrity in Indian gaming and advocacy issues in tribal sovereignty.

PUBLICATIONS: The monthly *Indian Gaming Magazine* in cooperation with the Public Gaming Research Institute.

Nevada Gaming Attorneys Association
325 South 3rd, Suite 1-310
Las Vegas, NV 89101

An association of attorneys that holds regular seminars covering developments in casino gaming law.

PUBLICATIONS: A newsletter entitled *Nevada Gaming Counsel*.

North American Association of State and Provincial Lotteries
1726 M Street, NW
Washington, DC 20036
(202) 223-4223

An organization of government lottery directors that conducts meetings to exchange information on security, internal controls, and marketing of lottery products. The association also assists new jurisdictions that wish to establish lotteries.

PUBLICATIONS: An annual report and directory.

North American Gaming Regulators Association
766 NBC Center
Lincoln, NE 68508
(402) 474-4261

A council of government officials and industry participants that conducts research utilizing existing state or provincial regulatory staffs and holds seminars and general meetings for staff members.

PUBLICATIONS: A newsletter.

Public Gaming Research Institute
15825 Shady Grove Road
Rockville, MD 20850
(301) 330-7600

This institute holds industry seminars and trade shows.

PUBLICATIONS: A series of magazines, including *Casino Gaming, Public Gaming, Lottery Journal,* and *Indian Gaming Magazine* (with the National Indian Gaming Association).

Race Track Industry Program
College of Agriculture
University of Arizona
Tucson, AZ 85721
(602) 621-4639

This university organization conducts seminars and short courses for the horse- and dog-racing industries. It also collects and disseminates information to interested parties.

Racetracks of Canada, Inc.
80 Bloor Street, West
Toronto, Ontario
Canada M5S 2V1
(416) 964-7976

An association focusing on information exchange related to the security, marketing, and financial operations of horse tracks.

PUBLICATIONS: A monthly magazine called *Track Talk.*

Special Collections Library, University of Nevada, Las Vegas
4505 Maryland Parkway
Las Vegas, NV 89154
(702) 895-3252

This library houses the world's largest publicly accessible collection of gambling books and materials. Materials may be used at the library site only; however, the library responds to telephone inquiries.

Thoroughbred Racing Associations
3000 Marcus Avenue, Suite 2W4
Lake Success, NY 11042
(516) 328-2660

The organization of racing associations advances the cause of racing through governmental relations and dissemination of public information. It adopts a code of standards for the industry. A subsidiary organization, the Thoroughbred Racing Protective Bureau, seeks to prevent corruption in the industry through investigations and records of track offenses.

United States Trotting Association
750 Michigan Avenue
Columbus, OH 43215
(614) 224-2291

This organization maintains the registry for all standardbred racing horses.

PUBLICATIONS: The monthly magazine *Hoofbeats* and the registry for standardbred horses.

Government Organizations

Alberta Gaming Commission
Browniee Bldg. 10365 97th Street
Edmonton, Alberta
Canada T5J 3W7
(403) 427-9796

Alberta Racing Commission
P.O. Box 5684, Station A
Calgary, Alberta
Canada T2H 1Y2
(403) 297-6551

Arizona Department of Racing
800 West Washington, Room 515
Phoenix, AZ 85007
(602) 542-5151

Arizona Lottery
4740 East University Drive
Phoenix, AZ 85034
(602) 829-7425

Arizona Racing Commission
P.O. Box 10539
Phoenix, AZ 85064
(602) 277-1800

Atlantic Lottery Corporation
770 St. George Boulevard
P.O. Box 5500
Moncton, New Brunswick
Canada E1C 8W6
(506) 853-5800

British Columbia Gaming Commission
848 Courtney Street, 2nd Floor
Victoria, British Columbia
Canada V8V 1X4
(604) 356-2797

British Columbia Lottery Corporation
74 West Seymour Street
Kamloops, British Columbia
Canada V2C 1E2
(604) 828-5500

California Horse Racing Board
1010 Hurley Way, Room 190
Sacramento, CA 95825
(916) 920-7178

California State Lottery
600 North Tenth Street
Sacramento, CA 95814
(916) 323-7095

Colorado Limited Gaming Control Commission
Department of Revenue
1375 Sherman
Denver, CO 80203
(303) 757-7555

Colorado Lottery
201 West 8th Street, Suite 600
Pueblo, CO 81002
(800) 283-5825

Connecticut State Lottery
P.O. Box 11424, Russell Road
Newington, CT 06111
(203) 667-9989

DC Lottery & Charitable Games Control Board
2101 M. L. King Jr. SE
Washington, DC 20020
(202) 433-7900

Delaware Harness Racing Commission
Dept. of Agriculture
2320 South Dupont Hwy.
Dover, DE 19901
(302) 736-4811

Delaware State Lottery
Blue Hen Mall, Suite 202
Dover, DE 19901
(302) 739-5291

Delaware Thoroughbred Racing Commission
820 French Street, 3rd Level
Wilmington, DE 19801
(302) 571-3288

Florida Division of Pari-Mutuel Wagering
8405 NW 53rd Street
Suite 240
Miami, FL 33166
(305) 377-7015

Florida Lottery
250 Marriott Drive
Tallahassee, FL 32301
(904) 487-7725

Greene County Racing Commission
P.O. Box 542
Eutaw, AL 35462
(205) 372-4213

Georgia Lottery Commission
230 Peachtree Street, NW, Suite 250
Atlanta, GA 30303
(405) 577-0600

Idaho Lottery
1199 Shoreline Drive
Boise, ID 83702
(208) 334-2600

Idaho State Horse Racing Commission
6133 Corporal Lane
Boise, ID 83704
(208) 327-7105

Illinois Gaming Board
State Office Complex
Springfield, IL 62706
(217) 524-0226

Illinois Racing Board
100 West Randolph, Suite 11-100
Chicago, IL 60601
(312) 814-2600

Illinois State Lottery
201 East Madison
Springfield, IL 62794-9080
(217) 524-5155

Indiana Lottery
201 South Capitol Avenue, Suite 1100
Indianapolis, IN 46225
(317) 955-6886

Iowa Lottery
2015 Grand Avenue
Des Moines, IA 60312
(515) 281-7900

Iowa Racing & Gaming Commission
Lucas State Office Bldg.
Des Moines, IA 50319
(515) 281-7352

Kansas State Lottery
128 North Kansas Avenue
Topeka, KS 66603
(913) 296-5708

Kentucky Harness Racing Commission
4063 Iron Works Pike
P.O. Box 1080
Lexington, KY 40588
(606) 254-7021

Kentucky Lottery Corporation
2 Paragon Center
6949 Dutchman's Lane, Suite 400
Louisville, KY 40205
(800) 477-7700

**Loto-Quebec Societe des loteries
et coursed du Quebec**
500 Sherbrooke ouest Bureau 2000
Montreal, Quebec
Canada H3A 3G6
(514) 282-8000

**Louisiana Economic Development
Gaming Corporation**
Louisiana Gaming Enforcement Division
Department of Public Safety
P.O. Box 66614
Baton Rougue, LA 70896
(504) 925-4799

Louisiana Lottery Corporation
P.O. Box 90008
Baton Rouge, LA 70879
(504) 297-2000

Maine State Lottery Commission
219 Capitol Street
State House Station #30
Augusta, ME 04333
(207) 624-6700

Maine State Harness Racing Commission
State House Station #28
Augusta, ME 04333
(207) 289-3221

Manitoba Horse Racing Commission
Box 40, Postal Station A
Winnipeg, Manitoba
Canada R3K 1Z9
(204) 885-7770

Manitoba Lottery Corporation
830 Empress Street
Winnipeg, Manitoba
Canada R3G 3H3
(204) 967-2638

Maryland State Lottery
6776 Reisertown Road, Suite 204
Baltimore, MD 21215
(410) 764-5770

Maryland State Racing Commission
Stanbalt Bldg, 14th Floor
501 St. Paul Place
Baltimore, MD 21202
(301) 333-6267

Massachusetts State Lottery Commission
15 Rockdale Street
Braintree, MA 02184
(617) 849-5555

Michigan Bureau of State Lottery
101 East Hillsdale
P.O. Box 30023
Lansing, MI 48909
(519) 335-5640

Michigan, Office of the Racing Commissioner
37650 Professional Center Drive, 105A
Livonia, MI 48154
(313) 462-2400

Minnesota Lottery
2645 Long Lake Road
Roseville, MN 55113
(612) 635-8228

Minnesota Racing Commission
11100 West 78th Street, Suite 201
Eden Prairie, MN 55344
(612) 341-7563

Mississippi Gaming Commission
P.O. Box 23577
Jackson, MS 39225-3577
(601) 354-6052

Missouri State Lottery Commission
P.O. Box 1603
Jefferson City, MO 65102
(314) 751-4050

Montana Board of Horse Racing
1520 East 6th Avenue
Helena, MT 59620
(406) 444-4287

Nebraska State Fair
P.O. Box 81228
Lincoln, NE 68501
(402) 474-5371

Nevada Gaming Commission
1150 East Williams
Carson City, NV 89710
(702) 687-6500

(Nevada) State Gaming Control Board
1150 East Williams
Carson City, NV 89710
(702) 687-6500

New Hampshire Pari-Mutuel Commission
244 North Main Street
3rd Floor, Carrigain Commons
Concord, NH 03301
(603) 271-2158

New Hampshire Sweepstakes Commission
Fort Eddy Road
Concord, NH 03301
(603) 271-3391

New Jersey Casino Control Commission
3131 Princeton Pike Office Park Building #5, C.N. 208
Trenton, NJ 08625
(609) 530-4900

New Jersey Division of Gaming Enforcement
Richard J. Justice Complex, Box C.N. 047
Trenton, NJ 08625
(609) 292-9394

New Jersey State Lottery Commission
Box C.N. 041
Trenton, NJ 08625
(609) 599-5800

New Mexico State Racing Commission
P.O. Box 8576 Highland Station
Albuquerque, NM 87198
(505) 841-4644

New York State Lottery
One Broadway Center, Box 7500
Schenectady, NY 12301-7500
(518) 388-3300

New York State Racing and Wagering Board
400 Broome Street
New York, NY 10013
(212) 219-4188

Ohio Lottery Commission
615 West Superior Avenue
Cleveland, OH 44113
(216) 787-3200 X223

Oklahoma Horse Racing Commission
6501 North Broadway, Suite 180
Oklahoma City, OK 73116
(405) 848-0404

Ontario Lottery Corporation
2 Floor Street, West, Suite 2400
Toronto, Ontario
Canada M4W 38H
(416) 961-6262

Ontario Racing Commission
180 Dundas Street, West, 14th Floor
Toronto, Ontario
Canada M5G 1Z8
(416) 963-0520

Oregon Lottery
2767 22nd Street, SE
P.O. Box 12649
Salem, OR 97309
(503) 378-3545

Oregon Racing Commission
1400 SW 5th Avenue
113 State Office Building
Portland, OR 97201
(503) 229-5820

Pennsylvania Harness Racing Commission
2301 North Cameron Street
Harrisburg, PA 17110
(717) 787-5196

Pennsylvania State Horse Racing Commission
2301 North Cameron Street, Room 304
Dept. of Agriculture
Harrisburg, PA 17110
(717) 787-1942

Pennsylvania State Lottery
2850 Turnpike Industrial Drive
Middletown, PA 17057
(717) 986-4699

Rhode Island Lottery
1425 Pontiac Avenue
Cranston, RI 02920
(401) 463-6500

South Dakota Commission on Gaming
118 East Missouri
Pierre, SD 57501
(605) 773-6050

South Dakota Lottery
207 East Capitol, Suite 200
Pierre, SD 57501
(605) 773-5770

South Dakota Racing Commission
118 West Capitol Avenue
Pierre, SD 57501
(605) 773-3179

Suffolk Regional Off-Track Betting Corporation
5 David's Drive
Hauppauge, NY 11788
(516) 434-4500

Texas Lottery Division
P.O. Box 13528
Austin, TX 78711-9939
(800) 375-6886

Vermont State Lottery Commission
P.O. Box 420
South Barren, VT 05670
(802) 828-2274

Virginia Lottery
P.O. Box 4689
Richmond, VA 23220
(804) 367-9444

Washington State Lottery
814 Fourth Avenue
P.O. Box 9770
Olympia, WA 98504
(206) 753-1412

West Virginia Lottery Commission
312 MacCorkie Avenue, SE
Charleston, WV 25327
(304) 558-0500

Western Canada Lottery Corporation
125 Garry Street
Winnipeg, Manitoba
Canada R3C 4J1
(204) 942-8217

Western Regional Off-Track Betting Corporation
700 Ellicott Street
Batavia, NY 14020
(716) 343-1423

Wisconsin Lottery
1802 West Beltline Hwy.
P.O. Box 8941
Madison, WI 53708
(414) 929-2063

Wisconsin Racing Board
150 East Gilman Street
P.O. Box 7975
Madison, WI 53707
(608) 276-3291

Wyoming Pari-Mutuel Commission
2301 Central Avenue
Barrett Bldg., 3rd Floor
Cheyenne, WY 82002
(307) 777-5887

6

Selected Print Resources

Documents and Government Reports

Governments in North America have issued studies and reports on gambling for more than a century and a half. These studies have focused on all aspects of the phenomenon, as discussed in the earlier chapters of this book.

One of the first government reports was presented to the public by the Committee of Twenty-Four Citizens of the City of Richmond, Virginia in 1833. A committee majority felt that the evils of gambling in the fair city could be overcome only with total legal suppression. However, three committee members dissented and issued their own report, which called for deliberate licensing of one or more gambling houses. With limited legalization, the minority's report stated that gambling could be controlled and its evil contained, but total suppression could never be effective.

The debate has continued ever since, and opinions remain divided on how to manage gambling in society. Below are just a few selected government studies and reports on this controversial topic.

Abrahamson, Mark, and John Wright. **Gambling in Connecticut: A Research Report.** Storrs, CT: Connecticut State Commission on Special Revenues, 1977.

This report presents a study based upon a survey of Connecticut residents and an examination of gaming literature. The authors conclude that legalized gambling will not lead to massive compulsions, but that gambling taxes will be regressive. They see legalization as a deterrent to some illegal activity, but not as an ironclad barricade to criminal elements.

Abrams, Robert. **Report of Attorney General Robert Abrams in Opposition to Legalized Casino Gambling in New York State.** Albany, NY: State of New York, 1981.

This report is credited with stopping a casino movement in New York State. Attorney General Abrams makes a scathing attack on the integrity of the Atlantic City casino industry, suggesting that similar problems of organized crime and political corruption would face New York if casinos were legalized.

Beare, Margaret, and Howard Hampton. **Legalized Gambling: An Overview.** A Report of the Solicitor General of Canada. Ottawa, Ontario: Ministry Secretariat, 1984. (Report 1983-13).

Beare and Hampton present an in-depth study of casino, lottery, race track, and off-track betting in the Canadian provinces. They also compare their findings with gaming operations in other jurisdictions.

British Columbia Gaming Commission. **The Status of Gaming in British Columbia.** A Report to the Attorney General by the British Columbia Gaming Commission. Victoria, BC: Queen's Printer, 1988.

This report presents a comprehensive overview of legalized gambling in the province. It examines the history gambling in British Columbia and the philosophy and social structure of provincial gaming.

Commission on the Review of the National Policy Toward Gambling. **Gambling in America: Final Report.** Washington, DC: GPO, 1976.

Congress created this commission with the Organized Crime Control Act of 1970. The commission gathered a wide range of information from 1974 through 1976. They concluded that gambling was inevitable and recommended that it be controlled by state and local governments. The commission also suggested that winnings from legal games not be taxed and that casinos be privately owned and located in remote areas away from city populations.

―――. **Gambling in America: Final Report, Appendix 1.** Staff and Consultant Papers, Model Statues, Bibliography, Correspondence. Washington, DC: GPO, 1976.

This 1,397-page volume offers expert views on all apects of gambling. Included is an 80-page report on the views of major religious organizations.

―――. **Gambling in America: Final Report, Appendix 2.** Survey of American Attitudes and Behavior. Washington, DC: GPO, 1976.

This volume reports results of the first comprehensive national survey on gambling behavior. The survey was conducted in 1975 by the University of Michigan Survey Research Center for the commission.

————. **Gambling in America: Final Report, Appendix 3.** Summaries of Commission Hearings. Washington, DC: GPO, 1976.

Between 3 April 1974 and 23 September 1976 the commission held 37 days of hearings and received testimonies from over 265 witnesses. This volume summarizes those testimonies.

Societe d'exploitation des lotteries et courses du Quebec (Loto Quebec). **Casinos.** Summary of the Final Report. Montreal, Quebec: Loto Quebec, 1978.

Quebec has been considering the legalization of casinos since New Jersey voters approved gambling in 1976. This initial provincial study recommended serious consideration of a "European Style" casino that has restricted membership (or entrance requirements), dress codes, and limited hours of operation.

State of New York, Casino Gambling Study Panel. **Final Report, August 1979.** Albany, NY: State of New York, 1979.

A panel of experts was appointed by Governor Hugh Carey in February 1979. The panel held public hearings, interviewed experts, and traveled to several communities with casinos. They concluded that casino gaming could bring economic benefits to New York State and recommended that certain communities be allowed to have casinos if approved in local referendum elections.

U.S. Congress. Senate Committee on Government Operations. **Report: Gambling and Organized Crime, March 28, 1962.** Washington, DC: GPO, 1962.

This committee, chaired by Senator John McClellan, investigated organized crime connections to gambling at the request of Attorney General Robert F. Kennedy. It focused largely on the use of interstate telephone lines to assist illegal gamblers. The report recommends that wire tap evidence be used in the fight against illegal gambling.

Books

Abt, Vicki, James Smith, and Eugene Christiansen. **The Business of Risk: Commercial Gambling in Mainstreet America.** Lawrence, KS: University of Kansas, 1985. 286 p.

The authors closely examine the structure of casinos, lotteries, and pari-mutuels. The book describes the range of gambling behaviors, including recreational and occasional gamblers, obsessive-compulsive gamblers, and professional gamblers. It pleads with politicians to examine the general public interest as they consider legalization questions. Attention to factual data is rigorous, as is the level of analysis. This is one of the most important academic treatments of the gambling industry and is valuable to scholars, politicians, and those interested in gambling as a public policy issue.

Allen, David D. **The Nature of Gambling.** New York: Coward–McCann, Inc., 1952. 249 p.

This is a dated survey of gambling, beginning with an anthropological and psychological consideration of the subject. The book examines the nature of gambling in many American states and foreign countries at the turn of the century. It is valuable for those interested in historical developments.

Asbury, Herbert. **Sucker's Progress.** New York: Dodd Mead, 1938. 493 p.

This is a very complete survey of all forms of gambling in America, from colonial days to the end of the nineteenth century. However, while jammed with information on games and personalities, the work lacks a focused point-of-view.

Barnhart, Russell. **Gamblers of Yesteryear.** Las Vegas, NV: Gamblers Book Club Press, 1983. 239 p.

Gaming historian Barnhart presents eighteenth- and nineteenth-century accounts of gaming enterprises at Bath, England; Spa, Belgium; Baden-Baden and Bad Homburg, Germany; and Monte Carlo, Monaco. The emphasis is on major personalities of the early casino era, including Beau Nash, Peter the Great, and Fyodor Dostoyevsky.

Berger, A. J., and Nancy Bruning. **Lady Luck's Companion: How To Play, How To Enjoy, How To Bet, How To Win.** New York: Harper and Row, 1979. 280 p.

An introduction to the full spectrum of gambling. Intended for the player, the spectator, and the interested citizen. Written in laypersons' terminology, it offers detailed and interesting facts about history, personalities, and gaming rules.

Bergler, Edmund. **The Psychology of Gambling.** New York: International Universities Press, 1958. 244 p.

This landmark volume portrays the problem gambler as a neurotic individual with an unconscious wish to lose. According to this work, the gambler habitually takes chances, allows games to preclude all other activity, brims with optimism, never stops while ahead, experiences a great deal of pleasure and pain while playing, and achieves his or her victories in masochistic forms.

Braidwaite, Larry. **Gambling: A Deadly Game.** Nashville, TN: Broadman Press, 1985.

This church-sponsored publication seeks to build a case against the spread of legalized gambling. The author examines forces behind the expansion, focusing on the Reagan Administration's shift of fiscal burdens from the federal to state governments and the emergence of a corporate presence in the gaming industry. Braidwaite believes that the legalization of gambling stimulates illegal gambling. The book examines lotteries, pari-mutuel wagering, casinos, sports betting, compulsive gambling, and moral questions concerning personal gambling behaviors.

Brailey, F. W. L. **Gambling in Canada.** Toronto, Ontario: United Church of Canada, 1958. 31 p.

This religious tract argues against gambling. It contains references to Canadian law and church edicts.

Cabot, Anthony, William Thompson, and Andrew Tottenham, eds. **International Casino Law.** 2d ed. Reno, NV: Institute for the Study of Gaming, University of Nevada-Reno, 1993. 565 p.

This is a collection of essays by various authors. Each examines the casino law of a particular country or political sub-unit of a country. Essays present historical information on the development of casinos, laws, and government enforcement agencies. The book offers a comprehensive body of information regarding licensing rules, taxation, and game regulations.

Campbell, Colin S., and John Lowman. **Gambling in Canada: Golden Goose or Trojan Horse?** Burnaby, BC: Simon Fraser University, 1989. 417 p.

This book is a collection of presentations made to the First Canadian National Symposium on Lotteries and Gambling, held in 1988. Similar to the United States, Canada has witnessed an explosion of growth in gaming. The essays consider the development of Canadian gaming law, lottery operations, horse racing, and charity gaming in various provinces and on Indian reserves.

Carroll, David. **Playboy's Illustrated Treasury of Gambling.** New York: Crown, 1977. 255 p.

This survey of gambling suggests that the activity is an appropriate recreational pursuit. Games are illustrated and advice is provided on how to play them.

Chafetz, Henry. **Play the Devil: A History of Gambling in the United States from 1492 to 1955.** New York: Potter Publishers, 1960. 475 p.

From land, gold, and silver rushes to lotteries for the Selective Service draft, America has always been a nation of gamblers. This is a very readable book which examines many aspects of our gambling history. Chapters look at colonial lotteries, riverboat gamblers, mining town casinos, and developments in horse racing. The book is packed with information, but lacks footnotes. A strong bibliography does make up somewhat for this deficiency.

Clotfelter, Charles T., and Philip J. Cook. **Selling Hope: State Lotteries in America.** Cambridge, MA: Harvard University Press, 1989. 323 p.

Clotfelter and Cook's comprehensive study reviews the history of lottery gambling and many of the public policy questions surrounding lotteries. The American public's overwhelming acceptance of lotteries is conditioned by powerful lobbies, which include suppliers and beneficiaries of earmarked funds from the activity. The authors see lotteries as methods for regressive taxation and as an acceptable means of raising money. They suggest that other forms of taxation should be considered as alternatives to the further growth of lotteries.

Coggins, Ross, ed. **The Gambling Menace.** Nashville, TN: Broadman Press, 1966. 128 p.

This collection of essays presents historical, social, economic, and psychological aspects of gambling with a religious slant. The well-written and well-documented articles are unsupportive of gambling. The editor accurately foresees a national drive for legalization. Evidently his plan to stop gambling expansion fell short of his goal.

Custer, Robert L., and Harry Milt. **When Luck Runs Out.** New York: Facts on File Press, 1985. 239 p.

The late Robert Custer is considered a pioneer in the development of treatment programs for compulsive gamblers. In this book he and Harry Milt present a comprehensive statement built around the medical notion that compulsive gambling is a disease. The authors examine the roots of problem gambling, phases of the gambler's career, impacts of gambling behavior on families, and treatment programs available for problem gamblers. The final chapter is devoted to the female compulsive gambler.

David, Florence Nightingale. **Games, Gods, and Gambling: The Origins and History of Probability and Statistical Ideas from the Earliest Times to the Newtonian Era.** New York: Haefner, 1962. 275 p.

The author ties the history of gambling to notions of mathematics and probability. The book discusses Galileo's experiments with dice, Pascal's use of roulette wheels, and Cardano's attention to games in a manner designed to make mathematics fun for the layperson. Nonetheless, this is a serious research work.

Davis, Bertha. **Gambling in America: A Growth Industry.** New York: Franklin Watts, 1992. 112 p.

This volume was published for young adult audiences. It provides a comprehensive survey of gambling enterprises throughout the United States. Specific attention is given to the pros and cons of legalized gambling, including issues such as taxation and compulsive gambling.

Demaris, Ovid. **The Boardwalk Jungle.** New York: Bantam Books, 1986. 436 p.

The co-author of *The Greenfelt Jungle* strikes again with an exposé of organized crime in Atlantic City. More fun reading, but again the story is one-sided and very selective. It does provide a good overview of the seamy side of Atlantic City's casino origins.

Dombrink, John Dennis. **Outlaw Businessmen: Organized Crime and the Legalization of Casino Gambling.** Ph.D. Dissertation. Berkeley, CA: University of California, 1981. 362 p.

This study examines twentieth-century developments in the casino industry. Dombrink devotes close attention to political support for casino legalization in Florida and New Jersey, emphasizing the central campaign issues of crime.

Dombrink, John, and William N. Thompson. **The Last Resort: Success and Failure in Campaigns for Casinos.** Reno, NV: University of Nevada Press, 1990. 220 p.

This book analyzes campaigns to legalize casino gambling in 20 states during the 1960s, 1970s, and 1980s. The authors theorize why the 1976 New Jersey effort was the only successful campaign while others failed. Failure to legalize high-stakes casino gambling occurred in states where government-run lotteries were being established simultaneously. The authors suggest that casino legalization efforts were subjected to a "veto model"—if one factor in a list of critical factors was negative, the campaign would fail. However, with lottery legalization issues, politicians and voters merely weighed the evidence. Using a "gravity model" they supported legalization if more facts favored gambling than opposed gambling. The series of factors included support from political and business elites, reputation of sponsors of legalization efforts, campaign financing, and dominance of economics as the key campaign issue. As the book went to press, Iowa and South Dakota authorized limited-stakes ($5) betting on casino games. The authors suggest that in the future voters may regard limited forms of casino gaming as favorably as they had lotteries in the past.

Dostoyevsky, Fyodor. **The Gambler.** Original publication date: 1866. Translated by Victor Terras. Chicago: University of Chicago Press, 1972. 164 p.

This is a novel (close to being autobiographical) about a compulsive gambler. Dostoyevsky often wrote to finance his self-destructive habits. His novel offers readers a very personal understanding of pathological gambling. Psychological motivations for gaming—including need for stimulation, feelings of social inferiority, and low self-esteem—are revealed, as are the physiological effects of the habit (trembling, sweating, imagined temperature changes). Scholars from Freud to contemporary sociologists have used the book as a benchmark for their studies of compulsive behaviors.

Eadington, William R. **Gambling and Society: Interdisciplinary Studies on the Subject of Gambling.** Papers from the First Annual Conference on Gambling, Las Vegas, June 1974. Springfield, IL: Charles Thomas, 1976. 466 p.

Proceedings and papers from the Second Annual Conference on Gambling, Lake Tahoe, June 1975; the Third Annual Conference on Gambling, Las Vegas, December 1976; and the Fourth National Conference on Gambling, Reno, December 1978, were not published in single collections. Individual papers are available through Special Collections Libraries of the University of Nevada at Reno and Las Vegas.

————, ed. **The Gambling Papers.** Proceedings of the Fifth National Conference on Gambling and Risk Taking, Lake Tahoe, October 1981. Reno, NV: University of Nevada, Department of Economics, 1982.

Thirteen volumes include papers on pathological gambling, the business of gambling, gambling legislation and regulations, and analyses of playing strategies, gaming stocks, and industry trends.

————, ed. **Gambling Research.** Proceedings of the Seventh International Conference on Gambling and Risk Taking, Reno, August 1987. Reno, NV: University of Nevada, Bureau of Business and Economic Research, 1988.

Five volumes on business activity, government policy, and playing behavior in the gaming industry.

————, ed. **The Gambling Studies.** Proceedings of the Sixth National Conference on Gambling and Risk Taking, Atlantic City, December 1984. Reno, NV: University of Nevada, Bureau of Business and Economic Research, 1985.

These five volumes cover gambling and public policy, economic issues, and pathological gambling.

————, ed. **Indian Gaming and the Law.** Reno, NV: Institute for the Study of Gaming, University of Nevada, 1990. 298 p.

Reservation gambling increased rapidly after Florida Seminoles initiated high stakes bingo games in the late 1970s. In 1987 the United States Supreme Court ruled that states could not regulate gambling on Indian reservations unless the games were illegal under state criminal law. The ruling prompted Congress to pass the Indian Gaming Regulatory Act of 1988, which paved the way for some measure of regulation over reservation gambling. In 1989 the University of Nevada sponsored a symposium on the new law. This book includes the papers presented there.

Eadington, William R., and John Rosecrance, eds. **Betting on the Future: Gambling in Nevada and Elsewhere,** vol. 2. Special Issue. *Nevada Public Affairs Review,* 1986.

This is a collection of essays on the gaming industry from a mid-1980s point of view. Two of the articles consider obsessive-compulsive gambling in Nevada; others deal with constitutional questions surrounding casino regulation, the competition of the California lottery with Nevada casinos, casino activity in Europe, and the gambling report of the President's Commission on Organized Crime.

Eadington, William R., and Judy A. Cornelius, eds. **Gambling and Public Policy: International Perspectives.** Reno, NV: University of Nevada, Institute for the Study of Gambling and Commercial Gaming, 1991. 688 p.

————, eds. **Gambling and Commercial Gaming: Essays in Business, Economics, Philosophy, and Science.** Reno, NV: University of Nevada, Institute for the Study of Gambling and Commercial Gaming, 1992. 656 p.

This and the previous volume contain papers delivered to the Eighth International Conference on Gambling and Risk Taking, held in London, England, in August 1990.

Ezell, John S. **Fortune's Merry Wheel.** Cambridge, MA: Harvard University Press, 1960. 331 p.

This is a comprehensive academic history of American lotteries from the early days of Jamestown Colony until the end of the nineteenth century. The author closely examines causes for the establishment of lotteries in many settings, as well as the decline of the infamous Louisiana Lottery. The book presents a mass of well-documented material and is a valuable reference work. Its lack of a basic theme, however, detracts from its merit.

Findlay, John M. **People of Chance.** New York: Oxford University Press, 1986. 272 p.

America was colonized by European adventurers, risk takers, and opportunists. Such people moved westward from the seventeenth to the twentieth centuries. Findlay explores the development of gambling against this frontier backdrop. The book concludes with three chapters devoted almost entirely to events in Las Vegas after the 1931 legalization of casinos. Findlay shows how the events reflect the broader culture of Americans as a "people of chance."

Fowler, Floyd J., Thomas Mangione, and Frederick Pratter. **Gambling Law Enforcement in Major American Cities.** Washington, DC: National Institute of Law Enforcement and Criminal Justice, 1978. 357 p.

This work reports on an intensive study of how police and prosecutors approach the topic of illegal gambling. The authors conclude that legalization is an ineffective remedy to the problem and concede that current enforcement efforts need careful review.

Frey, James H., and William R. Eadington, eds. **Gambling: Views from the Social Sciences,** vol. 474. *Annals of the American Academy of Political and Social Science,* July 1984. 233 p.

This is a valuable collection of research studies. Of particular importance is editor James Frey's sociological review of gambling and James Smith and Vicki Abt's examination of gambling as play. Also of note is Roy Kaplan's study of the social and economic impacts of lotteries. Other articles examine police enforcement of anti-gambling statutes, urban development and Atlantic City casinos, and the psychology of gambling.

Geis, Gilbert. **Not the Law's Business.** New York: Schocken, 1979. 262 p.

A comprehensive analysis of "victimless" crimes in America. Gambling is presented in the context of other such crimes, such as those related to alcohol and drug use, homosexuality, and illegal abortion.

Halliday, Jon, and Peter Fuller, eds. **The Psychology of Gambling.** London: Allen Lane, 1974. 310 p.

A collection of writings on compulsive gambling. Sigmund Freud's major study of Dostoyevsky is included. The book also offers a comprehensive bibliography.

Haskins, Jim. **Gambling Who Really Wins?** New York, Franklin Watts, 1979. 64 p.

A easy-to-read description of the gambling enterprise. The book concludes with a chapter about compulsive gambling, its treatment, and a warning to gamble safely and in moderation. However, the book deals only in generalities and lacks a plan-of-action for those desiring to recover from gambling problems.

Herman, Robert D. **Gamblers and Gambling: Motives, Institutions and Controls.** Lexington, MA: D.C. Heath, 1976. 142 p.

This book synthesizes the views of many academic scholars on the subject of compulsive gambling. The author also looks at horse racing and other gambling operations.

————, ed. **Gambling.** New York: Harper and Row, 1967. 264 p.

Although this collection was put together more than 25 years ago, the essays still hold value for today's students of gambling. Many of the articles emphasize social science approaches. Authors include Thorstein Veblen, William F. Whyte, and Edmund Bergler. Other articles on public policy include one by the late Robert F. Kennedy.

Hulse, James W. **Forty Years in the Wilderness.** Reno, NV: University of Nevada Press, 1986. 141 p.

Hulse says Nevada is and always has been the only state with the true character of a "company town." Once controlled by mining companies, today it is the gambling corporations that maintain significant influence in Nevada. Hulse says regulation of the industry by the government is weak at best. He traces industry development from the "mob" days, through the Howard Hughes period, to the advent of large corporations. Hulse perceives a need for radical change, which includes federal gambling regulation.

The International Casino Guide. 3rd ed. Port Washington, NY: B.D.I.T., Inc., 1992. 349 p.

Where are the casinos, what are their games, and how many tables and slot machines do they offer players? This reference book lists virtually every casino property in the world, along with information regarding currency controls, regulatory agencies, transportation, hotel, and restaurant facilities.

Johnston, David. **Temples of Chance: How America Inc. Bought Out Murder Inc. to Win Control of the Casino Business.** New York: Doubleday, 1992. 312 p.

For many years the author has been the gambling reporter for the *Philadelphia Inquirer.* As such, he reported on the manner in which corporations came to dominate political leaders in Atlantic City. The stories he relates here are as fascinating as those in Demaris and Reid's books, and are presented in a thoroughly researched manner. This book raises questions about how politicians can be as compromised by greed, as they are by members of crime organizations.

Jones, J. Philip. **Gambling: Yesterday and Today, A Complete History.** Devon, U.K.: David and Charles, 1973. 192 p.

Because this overview of gambling was written two decades ago, much of its material is dated. However, several chapters devoted to historical surveys remain valuable. These include histories of playing cards and animal and bird sports—subjects usually not covered well in other gambling surveys. A basic theme in the book is the notion that the gambling phenomenon has links with the early development of human beings. The early members of the human species had to risk safety and comfort everyday in order to secure food and the other necessities of life. The author states that a risk-taking genetic structure—inherited from our Adam and Eve—draws us toward gambling today.

Kaplan, H. Roy. **Lottery Winners.** New York: Harper and Row, 1978. 173 p.

Kaplan tracked down and interviewed winners of $1 million (or more). In this fascinating analysis he reveals that nearly three-fourths of the big winners quit their jobs. He views lotteries as governmental devices that aim to divert people from the banalities of their daily lives by allowing them to "dream the impossible dream."

Karcher, Alan. **Lotteries.** New Brunswick, NJ: Transaction. 1989. 116 p.

Karcher, a former New Jersey state senator, approaches the subject of lotteries from the perspective of a government official. He assesses the economic value of lotteries as public revenue sources as well as the dangers present in the marketing of lottery products. His final chapter suggests changes in lottery operation, which include increased payouts, restricted sales to minors and intoxicated ticket buyers, and bans on sales of gambling products over the telephone. Karcher also urges restrictions on lottery advertising.

Kefauver, Estes. **Crime in America.** Garden City, NY: Doubleday, 1951. 333 p.

United States Senator Estes Kefauver of Tennessee conducted extensive and well-publicized hearings on the role of organized crime in American society and concluded that illegal gambling was the major activity of the national criminal network. The book relates his impressions of the hearings in a sobering fashion and is designed to stimulate public outrage and indignation.

Kelly, Joseph, ed. **New York School Journal of International and Comparative Law: Special Issue on Gambling.** Vol. 8, No. 1, Winter 1986. 192 p.

Five essays detail the passage and implementation of casino law in Great Britain, British methods of gaming debt collection, gambling on the high seas, the evolution of gambling in Australia, and the impact of American law on casino development in other jurisdictions. The articles are thoroughly documented, and each is a useful resource for those desiring to pursue these topics more intensively.

King, Rufus. **Gambling and Organized Crime.** Washington, DC: Public Affairs Press, 1969. 239 p.

Attorney Rufus King prepared an extensive report on gambling and organized crime for President Lyndon Johnson's Crime Commission. Here he expands on the report by examining all aspects of crime and gambling. King looks at operators, the gambling utilized by crime networks, and the relationships between legal and illegal gambling, and suggests that these problems cannot be solved solely by local government. He also rejects the notion that legalization is a solution, pointing to the criminal involvement in legal casinos, and calls for the creation of a new federal agency with extensive authority to conduct wiretaps of crime organizations.

Kusyszyn, Igor, ed. **Studies in the Psychology of Gambling.** New York: Simon and Schuster, 1972. 172 p.

Kusyszyn offers a set of academic writings that were originally published in the late 1960s. Especially valuable are articles that survey various psychological findings on the subject of compulsive gambling and its treatment.

Lehne, Richard. **Casino Policy.** New Brunswick, NJ: Rutgers University Press, 1986. 268 p.

Richard Lehne examines the processes by which New Jersey engineered regulatory structures and rules for casino gaming after the state approved casinos in Atlantic City. Thirty elements in the Casino Control Act of 1977 are closely examined. The author assesses whether each was implemented according to the legislature's intentions. The analysis provides insight into the failures of Atlantic City to achieve the dream of urban revitalization.

Lesieur, Henry R. **The Chase: Career of the Compulsive Gambler.** Cambridge, MA: Schenkman, 1984. 323 p.

Henry Lesieur is the editor of the *Journal of Gambling Studies* (formerly the *Journal of Gambling Behavior*). In this book, he describes the developmental stages in compulsive gambling behavior. The problem gambler plays games early in his lifetime and experiences early big wins—wins accompanied by psychological highs. In subsequent career stages, the gambler is perpetually chasing bad bets with more bets of higher amounts. He is in a feverish quest to retrieve a new psychological high equal to that experienced as a younger person. This is "the chase."

Longstreet, Stephen. **Win or Lose: A Social History of Gambling.** Indianapolis, IN: Bobbs Merrill, 1977. 268 p.

Win or Lose offers an extensive body of information about games and gambling in the United States. While comprehensive in scope, the information lacks documentation. This limits the book's value as a research tool. On the other hand, for the general reader it merits attention.

Mahon, Gigi. **The Company That Bought the Boardwalk.** New York: Random House, 1980. 262 p.

Mahon's "Atlantic City" is the story of how one company, Resorts International, decided to enter the casino gaming business and how it manipulated political leaders in both the Bahamas and New Jersey to gain windfall profits. The book is an exposé. It is well written and documented by the author who is on the staff of *Barron's Magazine*.

Martinez, Tomas M. **The Gambling Scene: Why People Gamble.** Springfield, IL: C.C. Thomas, 1983. 231 p.

The author uses in-depth interviews as well as participant observations as he formulates a sociological definition of compulsive gambling. He looks at the progressive steps of the disease as well as treatment programs. He also explores the many social costs attending government promotion of gambling activities.

Moody, Gordon. **Quit Compulsive Gambling: The Action Plan for Gamblers and Their Families.** Wellingborough, U.K.: Thorsons, 1990. 144 p.

According to the author, excessive gamblers are vulnerable people. They are impatient, have active dreamworld imaginations, and are taken over by the action of play. Gordon Moody has worked for decades as a Gamblers Anonymous counsellor. Moody employs his personal experience in his discussion of excessive gambling. He explains the recovery path outlined by the Gamblers Anonymous program, specifically the 12-step method adapted from Alcoholics Anonymous.

Newman, David, ed. **Esquire's Book of Gambling.** New York: Harper and Row, 1962. 333 p.

This series of articles from *Esquire Magazine* covers many aspects of gaming—psychology, rules, and operations.

O'Donnell, John R. **Trumped: The Inside Story of the Real Donald Trump, His Cunning Rise and Spectacular Fall.** New York: Simon and Shuster, 1991. 348 p.

The casino industry has always been dominated by individuals. Once mob leaders dominated the scene, then Howard Hughes. Even after corporations took over, the role of the individual remained important. In the l980s three personalities controlled the Atlantic City casino industry—Steve Wynn, Merv Griffith, and Donald Trump. This book examines Donald Trump as a casino entrepreneur. It is laden with many anecdotes that challenge the image of Trump as a master of good deals. The book reveals many interesting sides of the business practices in the casino industry.

Parmer, Charles B. **For Gold and Glory.** New York: Carrick and Evans, 1939. 352 p.

This is the story of horse racing in America, from its colonial beginnings in Virginia to the Triple Crown races of the twentieth century. The author provides much incidental information on jockeys, trainers, racing officials, owners, and bettors. A collection of action photographs make it an enjoyable reading venture.

Peterson, Virgil. **Gambling: Should It Be Legalized?** Springfield, IL: Charles C. Thomas, 1951. 158 p.

Virgil Peterson served for many years as the director of the Chicago Crime Commission. As the city's chief "watchdog" over crime, he observed much illegal gambling. In response to many who advocated legalization as a means to cope with the illegal activity, he argues that legalization exacerbates problems of crime in the community. He finds that all gambling is parasitic nonproductive activity—whether legal or illegal. This 1951 book is especially valuable as a historical document that reflects the predominant perspective on gambling in the middle of the century.

Ploscowe, Morris, and Edwin J. Lukas, eds. **Gambling.** *Annals of the American Academy of Political and Social Science,* Special Issue, vol. 269, May 1950. 209 p.

This symposium of articles represents the first serious attempt to collect studies that provide an overall analysis of the gambling problems in society. Articles consider the legal status of gambling, the forms of games offered, the psychology of gambling, and gambling in foreign countries.

Pollock, Michael. **Hostage to Fortune: Atlantic City and Casino Gambling.** Princeton, NJ: Center for the Analysis of Public Issues, 1987. 204 p.

Pollock, a newspaper reporter, presents another chronicle of the Atlantic City story. This is a balanced account of the positive results of casino gaming and the failures of this experiment in urban redevelopment. The referenda campaigns of 1974 and 1976 are reviewed along with the steps taken to establish the first casinos. Attention is given to the early work of the Casino Control Commission, the role of organized crime in Atlantic City, and the effects of casino development on local housing and land values.

Reid, Ed, and Ovid Demaris. **The Greenfelt Jungle.** New York: Pocket Books, 1964. 244 p.

According to this account, the purpose of Las Vegas is to fleece money out of a gullible public. Reid and Demaris provide a one-sided view suggesting that Las Vegas is controlled by organized crime families and politicians who do their bidding. It makes for fun reading, as long as the reader keeps in mind that the story is slanted and that it was put together over three decades ago.

Robertson, William H.P. **A History of Thoroughbred Racing in America.** Englewood Cliffs, NJ: Prentice Hall, 1964. 621 p.

Robertson has written a detailed history of 300 years of horse racing in America. The book is an authoritative document that is both readable and a valuable reference tool.

Rose, I. Nelson. **Gambling and the Law.** Hollywood, CA: Gambling Times Press, 1986. 304 p.

This is a law book for the layperson. It contains a series of essays by Professor I. Nelson Rose of the Whittier College of Law. The chapters cover a wide variety of subjects including the organization of gambling regulatory bodies, the law of gambling debts, constitutional questions regarding prohibitions of advertising on gambling, IRS cash transaction reporting requirements, and definitions of gambling. While the book is not a tight-knit legal treatise, it contains many interpretations which merit the attention of those interested in studying gambling.

Rosecrance, John. **The Degenerates of Lake Tahoe.** New York: Peter Lang, 1985. 169 p.

John Rosecrance has been a participant observer of regular horse racing bettors in the racebooks of Lake Tahoe, Nevada casinos. In his book, he closely examines strategies for selecting horses for bets, for making the actual bets, and for analyzing the results of the races afterward. He finds that most gamblers are acting on a rational decision-making model as they wager—at least in their own minds. They deny that their behavior is compulsive or that they are out of control, even when their losses are excessive. The social structure of the gamblers' environment is offered as an alternative to that in normal society, yet in itself it is also seen as normal.

————. **Gambling without Guilt: The Legitimation of an American Pastime.** Pacific Grove, CA: Brooks-Cole, 1988. 174 p.

Rosecrance feels that gamblers should not experience guilt for gambling, which is quite normal behavior. In this book Rosecrance offers a critique of the medical model of obsessive gambling. He rejects the notion that excessive or problem gambling is a disease with only one remedy—abstinence. This valuable book presents a quick social and historical survey of the entire issue of legalized gambling.

Ross, Gary. **Stung: The Incredible Obsession of Brian Moloney.** Toronto, Ontario: Stoddart Publishing, Ltd., 1987. (Published in an American edition under the title *No Limit.* New York: Morrow, 1987. 301 p.)

Gary Ross provides the most insightful description of a compulsive gambler since Dostoyevsky's *The Gambler* was penned in 1866. *Stung* is the story of Brian Moloney. As a child Moloney went to the race track near his Ontario home. As a college student he served as a bookie for his fellow students. Soon after graduation he was working as a loan officer in a prominent bank. By this time he was "hooked" with the gambling disease. He had gone through the cycles of an early big win, chased by more and more gaming, and more and more losses. His work gave him opportunities for embezzlements. But instead of paying off gambling debts and quitting, Moloney just kept gambling. He discovered that casinos offered faster action. Casinos catered to his needs and pleasures with no thought about the source of his money. By the time he was caught, he had lost over ten million dollars.

Sasuly, Richard. **Bookies and Bettors: Two Hundred Years of Gambling.** New York: Holt, Rinehart, and Winston, 1982. 266 p.

This social history of gambling links today's American gaming enterprise to British establishments from the eighteenth and nineteenth centuries. The emphasis is on horse race betting and Mafia influence among bookies.

Scarne, John. **Scarne's Guide to Casino Gambling.** New York: Simon and Schuster, 1978. 352 p.

This is one of several guides to gambling written by a leading authority in the field. The chapters cover history, game descriptions, and observations on the operations of casinos. The author advises players on systems including card-counting methods for blackjack games.

Scott, Marvin B. **The Racing Game.** Chicago: Aldine, 1968. 186 p.

This volume treats horse racing as a social organization tied together by information systems. This academic book will be enjoyed by the serious student of gaming and the "sport of kings." Extensive references to other works on horse racing are provided.

Shaffer, Howard J., Sharon A. Stein, Blase Gambino, and Thomas N. Cummings, eds. **Compulsive Gambling: Theory, Research, and Practice.** Lexington, MA: Lexington Books, 1989. 350 p.

This book presents a collection of essays on the status of research knowledge about the problem of compulsive gambling. Special consideration is given to models of treatment. The notion that treatment demands abstinence is contrasted with behavior modification approaches. Actual treatment programs are discussed. The effect of compulsive gambling on family life is explored, as are public policy options for dealing with the pathological behaviors.

Skolnick, Jerome. **House of Cards: Legalization and Control of Casino Gambling.** Boston: Little Brown, 1978. 382 p.

This is a sociological analysis of casino gaming operations in Las Vegas. The author looks at the history of Nevada gaming, the operators—individual and corporate, the sources of financing, and the general public attitude toward such an industry. Especially valuable are chapters contributed by John Dombrink on gaming regulation and how criminal elements have compromised gaming.

Spanier, David. **Easy Money: Inside the Gambler's Mind.** London: Seeker and Warburg, 1987. 209 p.

A connoisseur of the gambling scene, David Spanier presents a very readable and enjoyable discussion of winners and losers he has met during his frequent visits to the casinos of Europe and the United States. His vignettes include portraits of Edward Thorpe, the math professor who popularized the technique of card-counting for blackjack players; Gordon Moody, the minister who pioneered gambling treatment programs for compulsives in England; and Marie Blanc, the grand lady of gambling at Monte Carlo in the nineteenth century. Spanier is positive about gambling, and readers will find his stories entertaining.

Sternlieb, George, and James W. Hughes. **The Atlantic City Gamble.** Cambridge, MA: Harvard University Press, 1983. 215 p.

A thorough account of the events leading up to the legalization of casinos for Atlantic City and the initial operation of the city's casinos from 1978 to 1983. The authors illustrate the successes and failures of legalization and conclude with a series of recommendations for other jurisdictions.

Teski, Marea, Robert Helsabeck, Franklin Smith, and Charles Yeager. **A City Revitalized: The Elderly Lose at Monopoly.** Lanham, MD: University Press of America, 1983. 191 p.

This study examines the way in which Atlantic City casinos changed the urban ecology for elderly residents in neighborhoods near the Boardwalk. The elderly had settled in Atlantic City because the decaying city offered inexpensive life styles. However, with the advent of casinos land values skyrocketed and investors began to crowd out the stores and shops which serviced the senior citizens. The authors suggest that jurisdictions considering legalization of casinos study Atlantic City closely.

Thorpe, Edward O. **Beat the Dealer.** New York: Random House, 1962. 236 p.

This is a classic account of how players can actually gain the edge on the casino by keeping track of cards as they are played in blackjack. The book resulted in a craze that has made blackjack the most popular table game in casinos today. It also led to casinos altering their rules to minimize "card counting."

Turner, Wallace. **Gambler's Money.** Boston: Houghton-Mifflin, 1965. 306 p.

Pulitzer Prize–winning journalist Wallace Turner turns his investigative skills on the legal casino industry of Las Vegas in this 1965 exposé. He examines the development of casinos capitalized with mob and Teamsters Union monies, and follows the flow of gaming profits from the hands of players into the hands of gangsters who engage in antisocial activities outside of Nevada. Turner writes that gambling is an immoral business given a "base of legality" in Nevada, and from this foothold gamblers have branched out to change patterns in American life. Turner's judgement that "gambling must be contained" is as relevant now as it was then, and he makes a case for federal regulation of gambling.

Vallen, Jerome. ed. **Nevada Gaming Law.** Las Vegas, NV: Lionel, Sawyer, and Collins, 1990. 352 p.

Members of the state's largest gaming law firm present an in-depth analysis of all aspects of the legal requirements for the gaming industry in Nevada. The book is a wealth of insights and understandings about the application of gaming law in the one state where gaming is the dominant industry.

Watson, Tom. **Don't Bet On It.** Ventura, CA: Regal Books, 1987. 249 p.

This is a religiously based book that presents the many negative aspects of gambling from a very biased viewpoint. Nonetheless, the arguments are presented in an organized manner and are supported by factual information. It is well referenced, and as such should be considered a good resource.

Weinstein, David, and Lillian Deitch. **The Impact of Legalized Gambling: The Socioeconomic Consequences of Lotteries and Off-Track Betting.** New York: Praeger Publishers, 1974. 208 p.

The authors have conducted the first serious socioeconomic study of two major forms of gambling. They draw conclusions that others are slowly beginning to realize: lotteries cannot solve the long-run fiscal problems of government, earmarked programs do not really gain from lottery funds, lottery funds are not stable government revenues, and government promotion of gambling can have negative social consequences. The authors outline a list of questions that should be researched by policy makers prior to legalizing more gambling.

Weiss, Ann E. **Lotteries: Who Wins, Who Loses?** Hillside NJ: Enslow, 1991. 112 p.

This young adult book presents a comprehensive review of the development of lotteries, their advantages and disadvantages, and governmental use of lottery funds. It is a balanced commentary which focuses upon the economic dimensions of lottery enterprises.

Periodicals

Casino Journal. Companion trade publication with *Casino Journal of New Jersey.* Editorial offices: 3100 W. Sahara, Suite 207, Las Vegas, NV 89102, and 2524 Artic Avenue, Atlantic City, NJ 08401.

Regular features of this monthly industry publication include articles on gaming law, personalities of the casino industry, casino promotions, and government policies in gaming. The journal is now in its sixth year of publication.

Gaming Technologies. Published by the Public Gaming Research Institute, 15825 Shady Grove Road, Rockville, MD 20850.
A monthly publication devoted to news and features about the commercial casino gaming industry. Formerly called *Casino Gaming International.*

Indian Gaming Magazine. Published by the Public Gaming Research Institute for the National Indian Gaming Association. 15825 Shady Grove Road, Suite 130, Rockville MD 20805.

This monthly publication began in 1991. It focuses upon gambling developments on reservations.

International Gaming and Wagering Business. Published by B.M.T. Publications, Inc., Seven Penn Plaza, New York, NY 10001-3900.

Started in 1978 as *Gaming Business Magazine,* this monthly publication is recognized as the definitive trade publication for the gaming industry. Its regular features include articles on lotteries, riverboat and Indian casinos, and marketing and customer service in the gaming industry. It also publishes the latest statistical information on all facets of the gaming industry worldwide and directories of gaming establishments and gaming industry suppliers. The periodical reports on new legal developments in this fast-growing industry.

Journal of Gambling Studies. Cosponsored by the National Council on Problem Gambling, 445 West 59th Street, New York, NY 10019; and the Institute for the Study of Gambling and Commercial Gaming, University of Nevada, Reno, NV 89557.

This is the only American academic journal devoted solely to the gambling phenomenon. Originally it focused on problem gambling and studies of treatment methods. In the later 1980s the editors sought out more general studies of public policy and gambling and changed the title. The quarterly journal provides not only the latest research studies into gambling, but also regular reviews of gambling books. Previously called the *Journal of Gambling Behavior.*

Public Gaming International. Published by the Public Gaming Research Institute for the National Indian Gaming Association. 15825 Shady Grove Road, Suite 130, Rockville MD 20805.

A monthly featuring news reports and stories about lotteries. Formerly called *Public Gaming,* the magazine began in 1973.

Turf and Sports Digest. Turf and Sports International, 118 West Pennsylvania Avenue, Towson, MD 21204.

Published since 1924, this bimonthly magazine contains stories about race track events and personalities. It features statistical records of leading horses.

Selected Nonprint Resources

Feature Films with Gambling Themes

HOLLYWOOD HAS ALWAYS REPRESENTED one of the greatest gambles of American life. Whether the player is a budding starlet from the Midwest, a playwright from the South, or a director looking for a box office kill, the movie industry holds the same allure as a lottery ticket, a long shot at the racecourse, or the spinning dice in a floating craps game. The glitzy town personifies a thousand parables of fame and another thousand hard luck tales. Hollywood has always been the story of good luck and bad luck and winners and losers. It is no wonder, then, that producers have sought out scripts that feature gambling themes or gambling settings. Below are listed 49 films that reveal Hollywood's view of the gambling phenomenon. Film descriptions are derived from Leonard Maltin's *Movie and Video Guide 1993* (New York: Penguin Books, 1992), from film reviews in popular media, as well as from personal observations of films. Each of the films is available on video cassette (VHS) while many are also available on Laser Disc (LD). Price listings are either from the 1993 catalog published by Wherehouse, Inc., or from the price listed by the distributor indicated (whichever was the lower). Addresses of the distributors cited are located at the end of the chapter.

Apple Dumpling Gang, The

Type: VHS/LD
Length: 100 minutes
Date: 1975
Cost: $19.99
Source: Wherehouse Entertainment, Inc.

A Walt Disney–produced farce that focuses upon the life of a Wild West card sharp who becomes the guardian for three orphaned children. The gambler takes the children into his world of deception and trickery, but then finds himself changing his ways as he accepts the obligations of parenthood.

Atlantic City

Type: VHS/LD
Length: 104 minutes
Date: 1980
Cost: $14.95
Source: Paramount Home Video

Burt Lancaster stars in this film, which presents a dramatic story about changing lives. It is set in Atlantic City in its early days of transition from a decaying resort town to a casino destination. The film portrays the town's traditional ambience as a haven for racketeers and gangsters unaltered by the onslaught of new legal gambling houses. Scenes include profiles of casino employees and their ambitions.

Big Hand for the Little Lady, A

Type: VHS/LD
Length: 95 minutes
Date: 1966
Cost: $19.98
Source: Facets Multimedia, Inc.

This mixture of comedy and tragedy is built around one poker game in the back room of an old Western saloon. A single hand of the game consumes an hour of the film. Different types of gamblers and their relationships are explored: the slick professional gambler, the con artist, the playful amateur, and the compulsive gambler.

Big Town, The

Type: VHS/LD
Length: 109 minutes
Date: 1987
Cost: $89.98
Source: Vestron Video, Inc.

A story centered on a young, small-town gambler who comes to Chicago in 1957 and continues his "hot streak." With his new bankroll he finds himself attracted to two women. He must choose between a wholesome, unmarried mother and a wild, married striptease dancer. Much of the scenery and plot are designed to make the film a 1950s nostalgia piece.

Billy Bathgate
Type: VHS/LD
Length: 106 minutes
Date: 1991
Cost: $19.99
Source: Touchstone Home Video

This very lucky man was the companion of Dutch Schultz in his many criminal operations, which included gambling ventures. Billy is just a young hanger-on who is drawn into a faction of the Mob just as the faction is on its ascendancy. The scenes reveal the interconnections between gambling activity and other organized crime ventures. A later falling out with his Mob benefactors leaves Billy Bathgate excluded from the meeting that results in the murder of his former associates by a rival gang.

Bob Le Flambeur (French)
Type: VHS/LD
Length: 102 minutes
Date: 1955
Cost: $39.95
Source: RCA/Columbia Pictures Home Video

This losing gambler gathers his friends together in a plan to rob the Deauville casino in France. The scenery displays the contrasting style of a typical European gaming house and the American casinos of Las Vegas and Atlantic City.

Bugsy
Type: VHS/LD
Length: 135 minutes
Date: 1991
Cost: $94.99
Source: Wherehouse Entertainment, Inc.

A fairly accurate account of how mobster Benjamin Siegel helped develop the famous Las Vegas Strip. This film offers glimpses of Siegel during his rise to gangland success, his interactions with a Lansky-like character during the establishment of the Flamingo, and his fatal attraction to Hollywood starlet Virginia Hill.

Casino Royale (British)

Type: VHS/LD
Length: 130 minutes
Date: 1967
Cost: $19.95
Source: RCA/Columbia Pictures Home Video

This is a James Bond spoof, with its many antics leading to the tables of the French Casino Royale. There Bond, an English gaming sharp, confronts a key executive of the spy organization, SMERSH, in a card game. The executive is a cheat, but he finds his match in his baccarat game with Bond.

Cincinnati Kid, The

Type: VHS/LD
Length: 113 minutes
Date: 1965
Cost: $19.98
Source: MGM/UA Home Video

This film features the game of stud poker, providing an excellent portrayal of the illicit professional gaming society in New Orleans—complete with the staging of a cockfight. The Cincinnati Kid, played by Steve McQueen, is a young derelict cardsharp who challenges Edward G. Robinson, king of New Orleans gaming, to a marathon dual on the tables. The activity develops slowly and methodically, giving the audience a feel for the emotion of the gaming.

Color of Money, The

Type: VHS/LD
Length: 119 minutes
Date: 1986
Cost: $19.95
Source: Touchstone Home Video

A good portrayal of pool hall hustling, an unorganized but popular form of gambling activity. The film is a 25-year-later sequel to the movie, *The Hustler*. It juxtaposes the differing life-styles between two generations. However, both generations are unified through their occupational life-style—pool hall hustling.

Deadly Impact (Italian)

Type: VHS/LD
Length: 91 minutes
Date: 1985
Cost: $29.98
Source: Vestron Video, Inc.

The movie is set in Las Vegas and Phoenix. In this farce, a young computer whiz develops a system to break casinos' central computer coding. He manipulates the messages on the computer chips, thereby controlling when the slot machines will have winning plays. After winning a large sum of money, he is hunted down by local thugs, and the film degenerates into a cat-and-mouse game.

Eight Men Out
Type: VHS/LD
Length: 119 minutes
Date: 1988
Cost: $19.98
Source: Orion Home Video

A careful study of the 1919 "Black Sox" scandal, which involved a gambler bribing baseball players in the World Series. The film records the social structure of sports betting and how players—both guilty and innocent—can be compromised if vigilant controls are not in place.

Electric Horseman, The
Type: VHS/LD
Length: 120 minutes
Date: 1979
Cost: $19.95
Source: MCA/Dome Video

Las Vegas becomes the setting for this metaphor of exploitation and innocence. The values of gaming life-styles and humanity are contrasted as Jane Fonda and Robert Redford team up to steal a horse from a Las Vegas show and head for open grazing land. The film offers excellent footage of Caesars Palace and the Las Vegas Strip, circa the 1970s.

Fox and His Friend, The
Type: VHS/LD
Length: 123 minutes
Date: 1975
Cost: $79.95
Source: Wherehouse Entertainment, Inc.

A carnival performer wins a lottery, but he discovers that his win has become a vehicle for his lover to expoit him. The film focuses on the issue of wealth and poverty and examines how the characters' mind-sets are altered by changing circumstance.

Gambler, The
Type: VHS/LD
Length: 111 minutes

Date: 1974
Cost: $66.95
Source: Paramount Home Video

This is not the Doestoyevsky story, but it is a story about a compulsive gambler. The central character is a college professor with an uncontrollable passion for gambling who will bet on anything simply for the excitement and uncertainty. The portrayal provides a valid case study of the problem gambler.

Gilda
Type: VHS/LD
Length: 110 minutes
Date: 1946
Cost: $19.95
Source: RCA/Pictures Home Video

The proprietor of a Buenos Aires casino becomes involved in a Nazi cartel. This intrigue serves as the backdrop for another story that occurs within the gaming hall. The proprietor's wife, Rita Hayworth, is also involved with a young gambler employed by her husband. Yet the plot strays off and is difficult to follow.

Godfather, Part II, The
Type: VHS/LD
Length: 200 minutes
Date: 1974
Cost: $29.95
Source: Paramount Home Video

As the second of *The Godfather* trilogy, this film features the Las Vegas connection to Mob families. The production won an Oscar as the best film of the year. Here the sons of the old-time Mob try to go legitimate by attempting to take over Las Vegas Strip casinos and manipulate Nevada politicians.

Grasshopper, The
Type: VHS/LD
Length: 95 minutes
Date: 1970
Cost: $19.98
Source: Powersport/American Video

A Canadian girl comes to Las Vegas with a dream but ends up as a wasted call girl. The film's value is in its portrayal of a side of Las Vegas society not outwardly observable in the gaming halls. Las Vegas shows illustrate the glitter that makes the Strip famous.

Grifters, The

Type:	VHS/LD
Length:	114 minutes
Date:	1990
Cost:	$19.95
Source:	HBO Video, Inc.

Scam artists work their trade until it destroys them. Many of their antics revolve around gambling operations including the slight-of-hand artist's scheme to win at the race tracks.

Guys and Dolls

Type:	VHS/LD
Length:	150 minutes
Date:	1955
Cost:	$19.98
Source:	CBS/Fox Video

The widely acclaimed Broadway musical about street lives and gambling in New York is brought to the screen. Frank Sinatra portrays Nathan Detroit—a small-time street player caught up in craps games and playing the ponies. Marlon Brando portrays the kingpin of the local gaming rackets.

Harlem Nights

Type:	VHS/LD
Length:	115 minutes
Date:	1989
Cost:	$19.95
Source:	Paramount Home Video

The film, set in New York in the 1930s, presents the story of an underground gambling club's owners' efforts to stand up to the Mob. Eddie Murphy wrote and directed this sometimes good, sometimes bad effort at comedy. The cast of comedy hall-of-famers includes Redd Foxx as a dealer with poor eyesight, and Richard Pryor, the casino owner "Sugar Ray."

Havana

Type:	VHS/LD
Length:	140 minutes
Date:	1990
Cost:	$19.95
Source:	MCA Home Video/Universal Pictures

Castro is about to take over, but a gambler decides to remain at the casino in order to make his last big win. As the game continues, stories of approaching troops fill the halls. Inevitably, the gambler gets involved in the political intrigue of the moment. The characters foresee the expansion (transfer) of gambling activities to other locales, including London, the Bahamas, and Las Vegas.

Hustler, The
Type: VHS/LD
Length: 135 minutes
Date: 1961
Cost: $19.98
Source: CBS/Fox Video

This is the quintessential film about poolroom hustling. Jackie Gleason portrays the legendary Minnesota Fats (see chapter 3). Paul Newman is the young pool hustler seeking his fame through his big time match-up with Fats. The action is gripping between the play on the table and the betting behind the players.

Jinxed!
Type: VHS/LD
Length: 103 minutes
Date: 1982
Cost: $19.98
Source: MGM/UA Home Video

Bette Midler stars as a Las Vegas singer who becomes involved in an adventure with a man who manages to jinx a blackjack dealer. Set in the casinos of northern Nevada, the film portrays the superstitions that control the life-styles of many in the gaming industry.

Kenny Rogers as The Gambler
Type: VHS/LD
Length: 94 minutes
Date: 1980
Cost: $14.95
Source: Wood Knapp Video

Rogers acts out the narrative of his famous song. The lines in the song give the basic lesson for the poker playing gambler: "Every hand's a winner, every hand's a loser." It all depends on how the hands are played. A winner's "gotta know when to hold 'em," and "know when to fold 'em."

Kenny Rogers as The Gambler, Part II
Type: VHS/LD
Length: 200 minutes
Date: 1983

Cost: $14.95
Source: Wood Knapp Video

More adventures with a deck of cards.

Kenny Rogers as The Gambler—The Legend Continues
Type: VHS/LD
Length: 200 minutes
Date: 1987
Cost: $14.95
Source: Wood Knapp Video

Rogers finally decides to "fold 'em" after a trilogy is completed.

Lady from Louisiana
Type: VHS/LD
Length: 82 minutes
Date: 1941
Cost: $14.98
Source: Republic Pictures Home Video

The crooked operations of politicians and grafters in the famous nine-teenth-century Louisiana Lottery are captured on film. The hero, played by John Wayne, is sent in to clean up the mess. The plot thickens as he is compromised by a romance with the chief culprit's daughter.

Le Million (French)
Type: VHS/LD
Length: 85 minutes
Date: 1931
Cost: $29.95
Source: Wherehouse Entertainment, Inc.

This adventure revolves around the quest to find a lost lottery ticket.

Let It Ride
Type: VHS/LD
Length: 86 minutes
Date: 1989
Cost: $14.95
Source: Paramount Home Video

This very humorous film looks at the world of horse racing and the gambling addicts that it attracts. Richard Dreyfus, like so many other pathological players, wants just that "one big day at the track." The film is shot at Florida's Hialeah Racetrack. The movie becomes a fantasy when Dreyfus gets his "big day" and somehow avoids gambling all the money back.

Little Vegas
Type: VHS/LD
Length: 91 minutes
Date: 1990
Cost: $89.95
Source: RCA/Columbia Pictures Home Video

A comedy about the Mob's efforts to invade the area around a trailer park and turn it into an illegal gambling retreat. The movie plays more like a poor television sitcom than a feature with the continuity of a real story line.

Lost in America
Type: VHS/LD
Length: 91 minutes
Date: 1985
Cost: $19.98
Source: Warner Home Video

A married couple drops out of the "rat race" and leaves suburbia to find America in their Winnebago. Their first stop is the Desert Inn Casino on the Las Vegas Strip. Quickly the couple's "yuppie" dream life comes apart as the wife gambles their entire savings away on a single stint at the tables. The film illustrates how quickly an innocent person can be drawn into pathological playing behavior. The film unflatteringly portrays casino personnel as allowing a compulsion to destroy people.

Lucky Luciano (Italian–French–U.S.)
Type: VHS/LD
Length: 110 minutes
Date: 1974
Cost: $9.95
Source: Nelson Entertainment Inc.

A screenplay about one of the leading mobsters who ran illegal gaming and other racket ventures.

Marrying Man, The
Type: VHS/LD
Length: 115 minutes
Date: 1991
Cost: $19.95
Source: Wherehouse Entertainment, Inc.

A carefree playboy goes to Las Vegas with his buddies and ends up falling in love with the casino mobster's girlfriend.

Mississippi

Type: VHS
Length: 73 minutes
Date: 1935
Cost: $9.95
Source: Wherehouse Entertainment, Inc.

The silver screen takes the audience back a century to a time when the Mississippi River was lined up with paddle wheel boats seeking to lure gamblers aboard. This musical comedy revolves around a riverboat captain and his poker playing. The ambience of riverboat gambling portrayed is in considerable contrast to the slot machines and polished felt tables of Mississippi riverboats today.

Monte Carlo

Type: VHS/LD
Length: 200 minutes
Date: 1986
Cost: $29.95
Source: New World Video

A spy story set around the classic casino. The film offers visuals of the Palace, which once stood above all others as the casino gambling capital of the world.

Naughty Nineties, The

Type: VHS/LD
Length: 76 minutes
Date: 1945
Cost: $14.95
Source: MCA Home Video

Bud Abbott and Lou Costello get into their comic routine antics on a Mississippi riverboat in the 1890s. The plotless script finds the comic duo operating with scheming businessmen and gamblers.

Ocean's Eleven

Type: VHS/LD
Length: 127 minutes
Date: 1960
Cost: $19.98
Source: Warner Home Video

This film offers a flashy look at Las Vegas, the tables, the slot machines, and, of course, the show girls. This comedy is about an eleven-man team that robs five Las Vegas casinos on New Year's Eve. The film stars Frank Sinatra and his "Rat Pack": Dean Martin, Joey Bishop, Peter Lawford, and Sammy Davis, Jr.

Pocketful of Miracles

Type: VHS/LD
Length: 136 minutes
Date: 1961
Cost: $19.98
Source: MGM/UA Home Video

Frank Capra remakes his 1933 film *A Lady for a Day*. As in the king of New York gamblers, Dave the Dude, always buys an apple from Apple Annie just for luck. When he learns that Annie's long-lost daughter is returning home, he decides to help Annie. The daughter does not know that Annie has fallen on bad times, so Dave organizes all his friends in a masquerade designed to convince the daughter that Annie is a society matron.

Queen of Spades (Russian)

Type: VHS/LD
Length: 100 minutes
Date: 1960
Cost: $39.95
Source: Kultur Video

This is a tragedy about pathological gambling. The film is set off by classical music scores by Tchaikovsky, which are performed by the Bolshoi Orchestra. A Russian army officer is torn between his love for an aristocratic lady and his passion to gamble. The plot focuses on his attempts to find out her grandmother's secrets for winning card games.

Rain Man

Type: VHS/LD
Length: 140 minutes
Date: 1988
Cost: $19.98
Source: MGM/UA Home Video

This film depicts Dustin Hoffman as an *idiot savant* whose mathematical skill helps his brother (Tom Cruise) beat Caesars Palace. Hoffman's mind is a computer machine that enables him to act as the ultimate card-counter at blackjack games. After achieving large wins, the pair is asked to leave the casino. There are some very good shots of Caesars, its gaming areas, and its other luxurious facilities. However, the Las Vegas setting is only a small part of the film.

Rover Dangerfield

Type: VHS/LD
Length: 74 minutes
Date: 1991

Cost: $19.98
Source: Warner Home Video

As a wisecracking dog cartoon character, Rodney Dangerfield enjoys his life hanging around the casinos in Las Vegas. Unfortunately, he is "dog-napped" and taken to a farm in the country. There he must learn to get along with new friends. However, he plots his return to the Las Vegas Strip and his old dog friends.

Run
Type: VHS/LD
Length: 91 minutes
Date: 1990
Cost: $19.99
Source: Wherehouse Entertainment, Inc.

A law student seeks out an illegal casino. While at the casino he becomes embroiled in an argument with the son of a mobster. In the course of a fight the mobster's son falls, accidently hitting his head, and dies. The gambling scene ends and the chase scenes begin.

Shadow of the Thin Man
Type: VHS/LD
Length: 97 minutes
Date: 1941
Cost: $19.98
Source: MGM/UA Home Video

The first scene is a racetrack. The betting action surrounds a mysterious murder and the plot thickens.

Stacy's Knights
Type: VHS/LD
Length: 95 minutes
Date: 1983
Cost: $29.98
Source: Vestron Video, Inc.

A young girl goes to Reno to try her luck at blackjack. She learns card-counting skills and, along with her boyfriend, she wins a large sum from the casinos. The casino retaliates by putting a crooked dealer into the game. The ensuing cat-and-mouse episodes result in her boyfriend's death. She then organizes her own gang of cheats and ultimately beats the casino. The card-playing scenes are mechanical and the overall flow of action is rather slow.

Strike It Rich (British)
Type: VHS/LD
Length: 87 minutes
Date: 1990
Cost: $89.99
Source: HBO Video, Inc.

An accountant gets caught up in gambling fever when he takes his honeymoon in Monte Carlo. The film offers another graphic study of compulsive gambling behaviors.

Thursday's Game
Type: VHS/LD
Length: 100 minutes
Date: 1974
Cost: $69.95
Source: Vidmark Entertainment

Poker-playing buddies commiserate about their business and marital problems.

29th Street
Type: VHS/LD
Length: 101 minutes
Date: 1991
Cost: $94.98
Source: Wherehouse Entertainment, Inc.

A venture about loan sharks and the winner of the New York State lottery. The film makes a good effort to illustrate how a lottery can cause many people to get caught up in a gambling frenzy. This is a very good action film with an interesting plot and a surprise ending.

Viva Las Vegas
Type: VHS/LD
Length: 86 minutes
Date: 1964
Cost: $19.98
Source: MGM/UA Home Video

Elvis comes to Las Vegas as a race car driver. He then gets into the musical business using Las Vegas as a set for his songs and his romance with Ann Margaret. Scenes include the neon, the tables and machines, and Hoover Dam. It is not a bad 1960s Las Vegas travelog. The plot offers Elvis and his music, nothing more.

Videocassette Documentaries on Gambling

The issue of gambling has been the theme of several documentary programs aired by public and commercial television organizations. The following list of such programs and other videotapes on gambling is taken from the Special Collections Department of the James Dickinson Library at the University of Nevada, Las Vegas. Because these videos are not always available for sale to the general public, price information has not been included. The distributors' addresses are listed at the end of this chapter. Inquiries may also be made to local libraries, as the tapes may be available through interlibrary loan systems.

Accent Las Vegas: The City of Destiny
Type: VHS
Length: 40 minutes
Date: 1985
Source: William G. Mors Productions

What is Las Vegas really like? This video looks at the history, educational system, housing, law enforcement, as well as the entertainment facilities and casinos of Las Vegas.

American Dreaming: Atlantic City's Casino Gamble
Type: VHS
Length: 52 minutes
Date: 1989
Source: After Image Media Productions

This video discusses the current attempt to revitalize Atlantic City, and examines the policy questions surrounding the use of casino gambling as a tool to solve deep-seated urban problems.

An Unauthorized History of the NFL
Type: VHS
Length: 60 minutes
Date: 1983
Source: WGBH Educational Foundation

Jessica Savitch discusses illegal betting, the role of the Mob in football betting, and connections between owners, coaches, players, and organized crime. Originally shown on *Frontline* on PBS.

Atlantic City: The Queen Takes a Chance
Type: VHS
Length: 60 minutes
Date: 1978
Source: New Jersey Public Television

Discusses the attempted rebirth of Atlantic City after the legalization of gambling. Interviews with residents and city officials.

Atlantic City: The Ten Year Gamble
Type: VHS
Length: 58 minutes
Date: 12 February 1988
Source: New Jersey Public Television

This program examines casino gambling in Atlantic City from its inception through its first ten years of operation.

Benny Binion Remembered
Type: VHS
Length: 45 minutes
Date: 10 January 1990
Source: KVBC TV, Las Vegas

A documentary on the life of Benny Binion, casino entrepreneur, developer of the Horseshoe Casino of Las Vegas, and founder of the "World Series of Poker."

Betting on the Lottery
Type: VHS
Length: 58 minutes
Date: 1990
Source: PBS Video

Discusses why people play lotteries and how much government treasuries benefit from lotteries.

Big Gamble in Atlantic City
Type: VHS
Length: 50 minutes
Date: 1986
Source: CBS Television News

Bill Moyers conducts conversations with major gaming industry players as well as citizens of Atlantic City in order to assess the accomplishments of legalized gambling in the community.

Compulsive Gambling: Against All Odds

Type: VHS
Length: 27 minutes
Date: 1983
Source: ABC Television

Discusses what a compulsive gambler is, and what help is available.

Compulsive Gambling: Betting Their Lives

Type: VHS
Length: 30 minutes
Date: 1983
Source: ABC Television

Focuses upon Gamblers Anonymous, GamAnon, and the treatment programs available at the Johns Hopkins Center for Pathological Gambling.

Deal Me Out

Type: VHS
Length: 28 minutes
Date: 1989
Source: St. Vincent's Medical Center, Richmond, NY

A docu-drama about a compulsive gambler, his struggles, and treatment.

Effects of Compulsive Gambling on the Marriage/
Can This Marriage Recover?

Type: VHS
Length: 43 minutes/23 minutes
Date: 1994
Source: Arnie and Sheila Wexler Associates

These two videotapes describe events in the lives of the two leading voices calling for the need to understand compulsive gambling in our society. They have both been there as addict and codependent. In the first video they describe the addict's downward spiral to ruin, and how that spiral of destruction affects family life. The second video records the long struggle toward recovery. Both are excellent educational videos. The cost of these videos is $295 per video, or both for $495.

Emerald River Resort: Paradise Found

Type: VHS
Length: 53 minutes
Date: 1990
Source: ABC Television. From the *20/20* news show.

The growth and development of Laughlin, Nevada, and the efforts to build the Emerald River destination resort.

48 Hours in Las Vegas

Type: VHS
Length: 52 minutes
Date: 26 January 1988
Source: CBS Television News

Hosted by Dan Rather, the show discusses gambling on sports and at casino games. Looks at the life of teenagers in Las Vegas, growing up in Las Vegas, and weddings in wedding chapels. Includes interviews with entertainers.

Future Vision Presents Poker Town

Type: VHS
Length: 25 minutes
Date: 1984
Source: Wombat Productions

A documentary on the World Series of Poker held annually at Binion's Horseshoe Casino in Las Vegas.

Horse Race Handicapping

Type: VHS
Length: 111 minutes
Date: 1984
Source: Jacada Publications

A college course on the business of pari-mutuel wagering and handicapping principles.

I Can't Believe I Won the Lottery

Type: VHS
Length: 60 minutes
Date: 1989
Source: STF Productions, Way Fun Productions, Fox Broadcasting Television Stations

Explores what happens to the people who win big state lottery prizes.

Las Vegas: Only in America

Type: VHS
Length: 52 minutes
Date: 1990
Source: International Video Network

This video discusses gambling and entertainment in Las Vegas, as well as the cultural diversity and history of the city.

Laughlin 1988
Type: VHS
Length: 53 minutes
Date: 1988
Source: KLVX-TV, Las Vegas

This video focuses on the development of a casino resort community.

Lucky Number
Type: VHS
Length: 57 minutes
Date: 1990
Source: Maryland Public Television

Explores compulsive gambling and treatment programs.

The Mob on the Run
Type: VHS
Length: 120 minutes
Date: 1987
Source: KLAS-TV, Las Vegas. Originally broadcast as segments of KLAS Eyewitness News.

An investigative reporter's history of involvement of the Mob in gambling in Las Vegas. Includes segments on Moe Dalitz, Allan Dorfman, the Teamsters Union, and members of the Atlantic City and Chicago mobs.

North American Conference on the Status of Indian Gaming
Type: VHS
Length: 800 minutes
Date: 1989
Source: The Institute for the Study of Gambling and Commercial Gaming, University of Nevada, Reno

Nine 90-minute tapes of conference speakers including members of Congress, Native American leaders, former Secretary of the Interior Stewart Udall, and other authorities on gaming. Speeches focus on the Indian Gaming Regulatory Act of 1988.

Statewide Conference on Compulsive Gambling
Type: VHS
Length: 300 minutes
Date: 1985
Source: Council on Compulsive Gambling of New Jersey

A series of taped presentations on topics such as crime and compulsive gambling, treatment programs, gambling and sports, and public policy on compulsive gambling.

Steve Forte's Gambling Production Series
Type: VHS
Length: 210 minute
Date: 1984
Source: Joint Ventures

Four videos expose various methods of cheating at casino card and dice games.

Distributors

ABC Television
77 West 66th Street
New York, NY 10023
(212) 456-7777

ABC Wide World of Learning
1330 Avenue of the Americas
New York, NY 10019
(212) 887-1735

After Image Media Productions
(no current location)
New York, NY

Arnie and Sheila Wexler
    Associates
1101A Beach Avenue
Bradley Beach, NJ 07720
(908) 774-0019

BTA Joint Ventures
P.O. Box 80876
Las Vegas, NV 89180

CBS Television News
51 West 52nd Street
New York, NY 10019
(212) 975-4321

CBS/FOX Video
Video Division(s): Key Video,
    Playhouse Video
1211 Avenue of the Americas
New York, NY 10036
(212) 819-3200
(800) 457-0686 (orders)
FAX (212) 819-3286

Council on Compulsive
    Gambling of New Jersey
1315 West State Street
Trenton, NJ 08618
(609) 599-3299

Facets Multimedia, Inc.
1517 West Fullerton Avenue
Chicago, IL 60614
(312) 281-9075
(800) 331-6197
FAX (312) 929-5437

Filmakers Library, Inc.
124 E. 40th Street, Suite 901
New York, NY 10016
(212) 808-4880

Fox Broadcasting Television
  Stations, Inc.
1020 West Pico Boulevard
Los Angeles, CA 90035
(310) 277-2211

HBO Video, Inc.
1100 Avenue of the Americas
New York, NY 10036
(212) 512-7447
(800) 648-7650
FAX (212) 512-7458

Institute for the Study
  of Gambling and
  Commercial Gaming
University of Nevada, Reno
Reno, NV 89557
(702) 782-1477

International Video Network
2242 Camino Ramon
San Ramon, CA 94583
(510) 866-1121

Jacada Publications
P.O. Box 1418
Louisville, KY 40201

KLAS TV
3228 Channel 8 Drive
Las Vegas, NV 89109
(702) 792-8888

KLVX TV
4210 Channel 10 Drive
Las Vegas, NV 89119
(702) 737-1010

Kultur Video
Video Division(s): White Star
121 Hwy. 36
West Long Branch, NJ 07764
(908) 229-2343
(800) 458-5887
FAX (201) 229-0066

KVBC TV
1500 Foremaster Lane
Las Vegas, NV 89101
(702) 642-3333

Maryland Public Television
11767 Bonita Avenue
Owings Mills, MD 21117
(301) 356-5600

MCA Home Video,
  Div. of MCA, Inc.
11312 Penrose Street
Sun Valley, CA 91352
(818) 768-3520

MGM/UA Home Video
10000 Washington Boulevard
Culver City, CA 90232-2728
(213) 280-6000
(800) 433-5500, Ext. 792
FAX (213) 836-9627

Nelson Entertainment, Inc.
Video Division(s): Charter
  Entertainment, Embassy Home
  Entertainment
335 North Maple Drive, Suite 350
Beverly Hills, CA 90219-3899
(213) 285-6000

New Jersey Public Television
1573 Parkside Avenue
Trenton, NJ 08638
(609) 882-5252

New World Video
1440 South Sepulveda Boulevard
Los Angeles, CA 90025
(213) 444-8100

Orion Home Video
9 West 57th Street
New York, NY 10019
(212) 980-1117

PBS Video
1320 Braddock
Alexandria, VA 22314-1698
(703) 739-5380

Paramount Home Video, Div. of
  Paramount Pictures Corp.
5555 Melrose Avenue
Hollywood, CA 90038
(213) 956-5000

Powersports/American Video
15700 Dickens Street
Encino, CA 91436
(800) 553-2030; (800) 338-2040
  (in California)
FAX (818) 907-0598

RCA/Columbia Pictures Home
  Video
Subs. of Columbia Pictures
  Industries, Inc. (NYC)
3500 West Olive Avenue
Burbank, CA 91505
(818) 953-7900
(800) 722-2748
FAX (818) 953-7864

Republic Pictures Home Video,
  Div. of Republic Pictures
  Corp.
12636 Beatrice Street
Los Angeles, CA 90066-0930
(213) 302-1656
(899) 826-2295 (orders)
FAX (213) 306-8865

St. Vincent's Medical Center
355 Bard Avenue
Richmond, NY (Staten Island)
  10310-1699
(718) 878-1234

Touchstone Home Video
500 South Buena Vista Street
Burbank, CA 91521
(818) 840-1875

Vestron Video, Inc.
Video Division(s): Lightning
  Video
1010 Washington Boulevard
Stamford, CT 06901
(203) 978-5400

Vidmark Entertainment
2901 Ocean Park Boulevard,
  Suite 123
Santa Monica, CA 90405-2906
(213) 399-8877
(800) 424-7070
FAX (213) 399-8877

Warner Home Video, Inc., Subs.
  of Warner Brothers, Inc.
4000 Warner Boulevard,
  No 19
Burbank, CA 91522
(818) 954-6266
(899) 626-9000 (orders)
FAX (818) 954-6540

WGBH Educational Foundation
125 Western Avenue
Boston, MA 02134
(617) 492-2777

Wherehouse Entertainment, Inc.
P.O. Box 2831
Torrance, CA 90509-2831
(310) 538-2314

William Mors Productions
407 Park East Way
Las Vegas, NV 89106
(702) 383-3041

Wombat Film & Video,
   Div. of Cortech
   Communications, Inc.
250 West 57th Street, Suite 2421
New York, NY 10019
(212) 315-2502
(800) 542-5554
FAX (212) 582-0585

Wood Knapp Video, Div. of
   Wood Knapp & Co.
140 East 45th Street
New York, NY 10017
(212) 983-8192

Glossary

baccarat One of a series of games (baccara, chemin de fer, punto banco) in which the winning hand of cards totals nine or a number closest to nine (tens and face cards count as zero). Two hands are dealt, one is called "the bank hand," the other "the player hand." Players may bet on either hand. In baccarat and punto banco all bets are against the house; in the other forms of the game the players may bet against each other.

banking games, non-banking games A banking game (or a house-banked game) is a casino game in which the bettor plays against the casino. These games include blackjack, roulette, craps, baccarat, and machine games. In contrast, non-banking games find players competing with each other. The casino is not a player in the game, although the house may charge a fee for conducting the game. The most popular non-banking game is poker. Pari-mutuel games are also non-banking games.

bingo This very popular charity game is usually played with cards containing 24 numbers (from one to 75) placed in five columns and five rows. The player purchases the cards before the game begins. A dealer then draws numbers one at a time randomly from a pool of 75 numbers, until one player covers a designated portion of the card with winning numbers—either a row, a column, or a predetermined winning configuration. That winner receives a prize. Bingo is generally conducted as a non-banking game.

blackjack Also called "Twenty-One." A card game where players seek to have a hand with cards totalling 21 or a number close to, but not over, 21. Players wager that their hand will be better than the house or dealer hand. The dealer gives each player two cards. The dealer also displays a single card. The players may then ask for additional cards in hopes of getting a 21 count. Aces may count as either one or eleven, face cards ten, and other cards their normal values. The term "blackjack" refers specifically to a hand with an ace and a single card with a value of ten.

card counter   A blackjack player who keeps track of all the cards that have been dealt. By doing so, he or she is able to calculate the odds of specific cards being dealt on subsequent plays. Expert counters can actually gain an advantage over the house. Certain casinos refuse to allow players to engage in counting techniques and ask them to leave if they are discovered.

casino (also called house or bank)   A casino is a location—usually a large room—where games of chance are played with some regularity. Today's casinos feature a variety of card games, dice games, roulette and wheels of fortune, and various slot machines and gambling video games.

chase   A losing gambler's practice of betting larger and larger sums of money in hopes of winning back past losses. This reckless kind of play is typical among compulsive or pathological gamblers.

chips   Tokens for gambling used by casinos to represent money.

chuck-a-luck   A game played with three dice. Players bet on whether certain combinations will appear after the dice are rolled. Variations of the game are called "Sic Bo" and "Cussec."

craps   A very popular American casino game in which players bet on combinations determined by the rolling of two dice. The specific term "craps" refers to a losing combination of numbers: two (called "snake eyes"), three, or twelve on the first roll of the dice.

faro   A very popular game on the American Frontier in the latter nineteenth century. Players make wagers on the order that cards will be dealt from a deck. It is basically a total luck game.

gambling (used interchangeably with terms gaming and wagering)
Placing something of value at risk in order to win a prize of value if a chance event (or an event determined in part by chance) occurs. The chance events are usually determined by the outcomes of card or dice games, contests, or drawing of lots. The legal definition of gambling requires three elements: consideration, chance, and prize.

grifter   A gambling cheater or swindler. Grifters use many schemes to cheat, including peeking, counterfeit cards, dice, or casino chips, as well as collusion with gaming staff members.

gross gaming win   The casino hold over a period of time. The gross gaming win is actually the amount bet minus the prizes given back to the players. This revenue won from the players is the basic amount utilized for most casino taxes.

handicapping   The activity of horse race bettors as they attempt to select (predict) winning horses. Handicapping involves the detailed study of performance charts for horses, their rider (jockey), analysis of track conditions, horse breeding, and other factors. Handicappers seek to eliminate as much of their risk as possible.

handle, drop, and hold   Handle, drop, and hold are terms used mainly in casino accounting. The handle refers to the total amount wagered at a game on games in a specific period of time. This amount includes prize money that is won and then bet again. The handle for a slot machine would constitute all the coins put into the machine in a period of time without regard to coins coming out as prizes. Drop, on the other hand, is the money the gambler brings to the game and plays. For instance, if a gambler brings $100 and plays the money at a blackjack table for several hours, experiencing both winning and losing hands, the drop is $100. The hold is the amount of money the house wins from the player over a period of time. For instance, if the player who wagers $100, leaves the casino with $80, the casino hold is $20.

hazard   A dice game that was very popular in England in the nineteenth century. It is considered the forerunner of craps and chuck-a-luck.

jai alai   A game played by two individuals or teams. Players use a scooped racket to hurl a ball extremely fast against a wall. The rules are similar to those of handball or racquetball. People make wagers on the winners, and betting in on a pari-mutuel basis.

keno (or Chinese lottery)   A game in which the player selects a set of numbers (typically one to fifteen numbers), and the casino then randomly draws 20 numbers from a pool of 80 numbers. If all of a certain portion of the numbers drawn match those selected by the player, the player receives a prize.

lottery   A game in which the winning numbers are determined by the random drawing of lots. In actuality, almost all forms of gambling games have characteristics of lotteries. In popular usage, the term lottery refers to government-run games which exist in two-thirds of the United States, all provinces of Canada, and in nearly one hundred countries. Lotteries involve the sale of numbers (or series of numbers) to a player, and then the drawing of numbers to determine which players are winners.

lottery, instant   A game in which a player purchases a ticket which has a concealed number (or symbol) upon it. A scratch-off variety ticket conceals the number behind a latex substance; a pull-tab ticket covers the number with a piece of paper. The player then removes the covering and reveals the number. If the number matches a predetermined winning number or symbol, the player receives a prize. These tickets are utilized by both government lotteries and charity organizations.

lotto   In the United States and Canada, lotto refers to a progressive lottery game in which the players select a series of numbers. The lottery agency then draws a series of numbers. If a player has all the numbers drawn, he or she is a winner. If no player has all the numbers drawn, the prize is added to a subsequent drawing after new tickets are sold. The prizes escalate with each drawing in which there is no winner. Some lotto games have had prizes exceeding $100 million.

marker   A slip of paper signed by a casino player when he or she borrows money from the casino in order to gamble.

numbers game   A lottery game in which a player selects a three- or four-digit number. If the number matches a number that is randomly drawn by the lottery organization, the player is a winner. This is the most popular illegal lottery game in America. Also called "policy."

odds   The advantage one side of a wager has over the other. In house-banked games, the casino will have an odds advantage in an actual game or it will have an odds advantage in the payoff structure used.

pari-mutuel betting   A form of wagering utilized for horse racing, dog racing, and jai alai games. All player bets are pooled together. Prizes are taken out of the common pool and given to those bettors who selected winners of the event (the race or the game). The gambling organization will also take a percentage of the pool as its fee for operating the game. Odds for prizes are determined by the patterns of players' bets. If many bettors place wagers on the winner, the prizes are small; however, if only a few bettors select the winner, the prizes are much larger. The establishment (the casino, house, or bank) does not participate in the gambling as a player.

point spread   A term used in sports betting to refer to the betting handicap given to those making wagers on underdog or presumed weaker teams. The point spread is used most often in basketball or football betting. As an example, Detroit may be a 7.5 point underdog at Dallas. Those betting on Dallas will not win their bet unless Dallas wins the game by eight or more points. Detroit bettors will win the bet if Detroit wins the game or does not lose the game by more than seven points.

poker   A non-banking card game which involves considerable skill in betting behavior. Players make wagers on which one will have the best five-card hand (although there are some games with other hands). Hands are ranked from the highest (a royal flush, that is, ace, king, queen, jack, and ten of the same suit) to the lowest in value. There are many variations in dealing. In stud poker, cards are dealt and the players must use the cards; in draw poker, the player may exchange cards for new ones. Betting occurs at the beginning (ante and opening bets) and as cards are dealt. In some games, some cards are dealt face up, in other games all cards are dealt down. In addition to being a casino game, poker is the most popular social gambling game in the United States and Canada.

punter   A term used most often in England to refer to a person making a wager. Synonymous with the terms player, bettor, gambler, or plunger.

raffle   A form of lottery in which numbered tickets are sold and then placed into a large drum or container. The players are given receipts for their tickets. The tickets are mixed up and one is drawn out in random fashion. The player who purchased the ticket is given a prize. Raffles are very popular in charity gambling.

roulette   A very popular casino game. It is played with a horizontal wheel with numbers from one to thirty-six and also either one zero (European Wheel) or two zeros (American Wheel) around the circumference. Bettors select a number or combination of numbers. The wheel is then spun and a ball is dropped into it. Eventually the ball settles in a slot beside a winning number. If this number matches the number on one of the numbers bet upon, the player receives a prize.

slot machine   A mechanical, electromechanical, or computerized device into which coins are placed and play is activated by a bettor. The machine displays symbols indicating that the player has won or lost the wager, and if the player is a winner the machine will distribute the prize (or paper or tokens as evidence of the prize). There is a wide variety of slot machines and video devices. The most popular video machines display poker hands and give the player a second chance by allowing another choice of cards. Today over one-half of the gross gaming win of casinos comes from machine play. Some state lotteries also utilize slot machines, which they call video lottery terminals.

win, place, show   Terms used in horse race and dog race betting. A win bet is a bet that a horse will finish the race first. A place bet is a wager that the horse will finish in either first or second position. The show bet is a wager that a horse will finish either first, second, or third.

Index

William N. Thompson is Professor of Public Administration at the University of Nevada, Las Vegas. He is a noted authority on gambling, has researched and written extensively on the topic, and has served as a consultant on gambling for national and international businesses and organizations.